# With Love, Karen

**John Michael Langley**

© 2024 John Michael Langley
TXu 2-430-252

First Edition
November 2024

ISBN: 979-8-218-39058-7

This story is a Bildungsroman based on actual events. It reflects the author's present opinions and recollections of experiences over time. Some names and characters may have been changed or combined, some events may have been compressed, and some dialog has been recreated. Certain characters are real, but their inclusion does not necessarily reflect their actual thoughts, feelings, statements, actions, or values.

*To Kasey, from Wheezer.*

# Table of Contents

# Foreword

It's a little appreciated fact that there are *Inner* and *Outer* circles around celebrity, and normally it's very difficult for anyone to ever break through to that inner circle. Most times deliberately so, and for a variety of reasons. Oh, to be sure, there are dozens, if not hundreds, of people inside the world of the famous; old friends, coworkers, agents, studio reps, technicians, even hair stylists. Some on a first-name basis, and many more who are not.

But what of the *regular* people?

There are certainly a few opportunities for us all to meet: autograph or photo appearances, perhaps even the chance of a handshake or a hug. But in these fleeting seconds, there is no *real* chance of a personal connection. These moments may be treasured for a lifetime by those who experience them, but for the famous, the exchanges are sadly forgotten the instant that they occur.

But this is the story of one regular person who, quite by accident, happened to enter the world of singing star Karen Carpenter. And from that moment on, both of their lives would be changed forever.

Based on a true story

# Introduction

It's just after 4 in the morning as I begin this story. This was always a special time of night for Karen Carpenter and for me as well. It's the time of night when each of us was often dragged from our sleep to try and resolve the problems and worries on our minds. It was so special in fact, that it became a footnote in a song once, a long time ago.

No doubt that many other people do this same thing, even if the exact time of night may vary.

But this small coincidence was to be the first of many that Karen and I seemed to share.

In a way it's a bit misleading to say that this is the beginning of the story because, in point of fact, the entire book itself is already complete. This Introduction was the only part left for last. It was the most difficult piece of the story for me to start, because it was the only part that Karen was not there in some way to help me recall — with one of the many memories of her that I have.

In the 50+ years that have passed since the earliest part of this story takes place, I've only ever shared this tale once. It was a month after her death. A framed photograph on a bedroom dresser was the trigger to a story that I never intended to tell. The person to whom I told it that night was the only one who ever knew, until today.

At the time, I thought that opening up about Karen might be a necessary first step in the grieving process that I needed to heal. But in looking back, it's a wonder that I was ever able to finish the story out loud at all that evening. In some type of reverse-grieving process, over the years it has only become more and more difficult for me to talk about her without becoming emotionally overwhelmed. And this has me concerned.

But at the same time, it also helps me understand some of the demons that Karen had to struggle with herself — the things in our lives that we do, even when we know on some level that they are wrong or even dangerous for us.

But as I approach 70 years of age, a new challenge has appeared on the horizon. The idea of losing any of these special memories has become more and more real, and more and more frightening. So I decided that it was finally time to capture this entire story in writing, so that a full and accurate account of our time together will exist, even if one final day, it becomes just an interesting new book for me to pick up and read in my old age, because my only remaining memory is of it "always being on my nightstand."

# March 20, 1983, 7 PM

"Well, that was really good," my sister Kathy said, as she got up from the table to help me clear the dishes.

"It was," I added. "I've been hearing good things about this place ever since it opened a few months ago. I'm glad too, I love Chinese food."

"I liked mine, too," Kathy's husband Bill said.

My sister and her husband were over this Saturday night to get together for dinner and a movie. I had rented "An Officer and a Gentleman" on VHS for us to watch. The take-out food part was my idea, so that no one had to spend a lot of time cooking or cleaning up afterward.

We tried to get together about five or six times a year, alternating between their place and mine. To be honest, as the day got closer, my heart wasn't really in it. But our last movie night had been cancelled due to snow, so I didn't want to beg off for tonight. That and I also thought it might do me some good to have company.

"I'll be back in a few minutes," Bill said, as he headed for the hall bath.

Kathy and I just looked at each other and smiled as we turned back to clear the few remaining dishes. Once we were done, I turned off the dining room light and we made our way into the living room.

"Oh, good choice," Kathy said, as she noticed the VHS tape on the coffee table. "I've been wanting to see this. Bill and I don't manage to get out to the movies as much as we used to when we were first dating. We missed this one completely."

"I remembered you talking about this film a few weeks ago. That's why I reserved it," I replied. "I have some ice cream for later, too, whenever you guys are ready."

"That may be a while. Bill ate all his food and part of mine!" Kathy laughed.

"The boy can eat!" I said with a grin.

"Before we get settled, can I use your bathroom to wash up? This finger food left me a mess," she said.

"They call them 'chopsticks'," I said. "You're not supposed to use your other hand to help hold the food!"

"Yes, well, we may want to revisit that one decision the next time we do Chinese!" she replied.

"Gee … " I said, as I thought about it. "I was running a little late tonight. I kinda skipped cleaning up my bedroom and bath and just closed the door to hide the evidence. Are you sure that you can't wait a few minutes for Bill?"

"No, I'd better not. I saw him grab the sports page as he went in. This may take awhile!" she said with a laugh.

"Of course," I said. "Follow me."

I opened my bedroom door and turned on the light, and as I stepped in I directed her toward the bathroom, just to the left.

"Pardon the mess," I said once again.

Once she went in and closed the bathroom door, I took a glance around the bedroom to see how bad it was. I quickly pulled both sides of the bedcover straight, and then grabbed a shirt and pair of blue jeans off my chair. I opened the closet and threw these into a wicker laundry hamper on the floor of the closet and closed the door. "Not too bad … " I thought.

Just then I looked over toward the far end of my dresser, and I did a mad dash over to there. I opened the top drawer, stuffed some things from the top of the dresser into the drawer, and quickly slammed it shut.

My sister was coming out of the bathroom just as I did this, and the noise of the drawer closing startled her.

"Everything ok?" she asked.

"Oh, sure," I said sheepishly. "I was doing some last-minute tidying up while you were in there."

Kathy just smiled as she walked back toward me and the bedroom door. Just then her husband came out of the hall bath, right outside my bedroom. She stopped, and we both turned to look out at him.

Kathy said, "We'll be right out hun. Why don't you turn on the TV and get things ready? There's ice cream in the frig if you want any."

"Oh, good," Bill said, as he walked away.

Kathy smiled as she turned back toward me. I was still standing at the far end of the dresser, near my nightstand. As she turned her head, the framed photo on top of my dresser caught her eye.

"Is this Karen Carpenter?" she asked.

"Yes, it is," I said.

"Oh, I didn't know that you were such a big fan!" she said. "She's so pretty."

Forgetting myself for a moment, I said, "Yes … That's my favorite photograph of her. This is more what she looks like every day, when she isn't being Karen Carpenter, the singing star."

My sister got a confused look on her face just then.

"What do you mean? You actually *met* her?" she asked.

"I did, yes … a long time ago," I hesitated for a few seconds.

"We were actually seeing each other for a short while during the summer of 1975," I said.

"You mean dating? I never knew any of this!" she said.

"No one does," I replied.

Just then she noticed the inscription on the bottom of the photo, and she picked up the frame to read it.

"This is made out to you and it says, 'With Love, Karen'. You're not pulling my leg about any of this, are you?" she said.

"No," I simply said, with a slight shake of my head.

After studying the photo for a few more seconds, she put the frame back on the dresser and said, "You sit right down here and tell me exactly what happened! This is amazing! My own big brother. I can't believe you never told me!"

We both sat down on the side of the bed.

"So how did you ever get to meet her?" she asked.

I took a moment to start.

"Did you ever have one of those experiences in your life, where you couldn't explain in a million years how it all happened, even if you tried?" I said.

Kathy nodded yes.

"Well, this isn't like that," I said.

Kathy just smiled.

"I can tell you in just two words how I met Karen," I said.

"Danny Betts"

# My Friend Danny

Danny Betts was my best friend through my teen years and well into my twenties. We went to the same schools together, hung out at the same Dunkin' Donuts at night, rode motorcycles together, and even worked for the same company. I was at his house as much as my own all through those years, and I knew both of his parents very well.

It was from Danny that I inherited my preference for luxury cars, versus the muscle cars of the period. For Danny, his car represented a lifestyle.

Danny could best be described as a John Travolta-like character from "Saturday Night Fever," if just a titch less handsome. But what Danny didn't have in total good looks, he more than made up for with a confident smile, excellent dance skills, and a smooth line of what can only be described as pure bullshit.

More times than I can remember, I watched him go up to girls and totally charm them over within five minutes, saying absolutely nothing meaningful at all, as far as I could discern. For me it was like watching some magician's slight of hand, never knowing how it was done, no matter how many times I witnessed it. I often thought that I should film the process with a high-speed camera, so that I could study it frame by frame. Danny called it, "Pulling a rap."

Danny also had the uncanny ability of looking at a girl from across the room and *knowing* with 98% certainty whether he would be taking her home that night.

I didn't have Danny's same bedpost skills or aspirations, but I will confess that I lived vicariously through watching some of his exploits, kinda like rooting for your favorite team. Don't worry, I won't attempt any "scoring" puns here.

It was from him that I learned the most basic of social skills around women — the ones related to talking and being comfortable, not the BS part — that I'd never master, even if I tried.

And thank goodness, for my sake, that Danny was a patient soul!

My contribution to this dynamic duo was brain power. I supplied most all the non-girl-related ideas that we had or acted upon.

I should probably stop right here for a moment to explain something to all those who bristle at my alternating use of the words "girl" and "woman." This is intentional.

When he had to choose, Danny liked them young, dumb, and pretty. Very pretty. Legal drinking age, or slightly older.

I dated women. Danny dated girls. I switch back and forth between the two simply to provide context.

But back to my contribution …

I often saw opportunity were others saw only chaos. It was late spring of 1973 when I persuaded Danny to come over and apply for a newly created job at the company I worked for. I sensed a unique opportunity that was a perfect fit for him, and Danny was soon earning twice as much money as he had been at his previous job by working for our firm.

During this time in America, it was still possible to leave school and make a very good living without a college degree. And even at that, our jobs were better than many. But it was an era that was about to come to an end.

But my greatest single contribution to the team was probably memory skills. Danny combined his artistry for BS with my unique memory to make what can only be described as a decent side income.

I always had something akin to a photographic memory, but I never thought anything of it. It was only after many, "What? You can't do that?" moments growing up that I even came to appreciate it at all, like remembering four ten-digit phone numbers instantly.

A "friggin steel trap" is how one friend described it.

How many times we'd be sitting outside of work on a payday, just having lunch and listening to the radio, and Danny would start talking about how he would bet anyone $20 that I could name the next song on the radio with just one note. And I did.

The reality was that I often had four or five notes as clues because the songs were still playing even as I named them, not that I always needed the extra help. But it still seemed like a miracle to those who witnessed it, all except for the unlucky few who took Danny's bet, like new employees, or truck drivers waiting for their cargo to be loaded.

After doing three songs in a row once, and Danny winning $60 from some poor soul, this fellow swore that he was being cheated. "You must know the station playlist," he insisted.

"No problem," Danny said. "Go ahead and change the radio to any pop station that you want, and we'll do it again. But if you do, we bet paycheck for paycheck. If John can't name that next song in one note, I'll give you my paycheck and your $60 back. But if he does, I get your paycheck and keep the $60. If not, then I'm just keeping this money."

Time to raise, call, or fold.

That unlucky fellow had some 'splainin to do that night when he went home with no money!

It was right after this last game that I reminded Danny not to get too carried away with the dollar amounts just in case I showed up tired one day!

After bilking all the rubes at work, his pitch soon moved to the bars, where he found a seemingly endless supply of new "customers." On a good Friday night, winning just $20 each from five different guys, Danny netted a spare $100 over the course of only a few hours. And this was at a time when the minimum wage was just under $2.

Danny was like my older brother, so I didn't mind helping him play these games. He always bought the beers, so we called it even. And it was actually entertaining to watch, because he did it a little differently almost every time. He was good at reading people, not just girls.

But at the same time, I also found that I was getting better and better at naming a lot more songs, with all this practice. I was literally down to just one note most of the time now.

My needs where pretty simple during those years. I had a nice car and my pride and joy, a 1971 Harley-Davidson

Superglide motorcycle. The Harley was a one-year-only red white, and blue machine that was toned down every year afterward to attract more buyers. But I loved it in its original form.

I wasn't able to buy one new, but I soon had a mint one-year-old bike with only 2,200 miles on it when I got it. This was my baby.

The good times at work ended for us between April and May of 1975, when my company laid off about 20% of its work force over several weeks. We were in the automotive parts manufacturing business, and it was getting harder and harder for U.S. companies to compete against cheaper Japanese imports.

The writing was on the wall for good paying jobs, as more and more of the machines at our plant were permanently shut down and their output replaced by container loads of goods from Japan. The company itself stayed in business and prospered, but it was the workers who became redundant.

Being a UAW[1] shop, all layoffs were done strictly on a seniority basis. Danny and I were among the second group to be let go, each of us having only worked there a few years. This lesson was a major takeaway for me, and I was determined to find a new career where my future and fortunes were decided based on my abilities, and not on my hire date.

---

[1] United Auto Workers union.

I saw computers and computer programming as that future. I did some research and was soon enrolled in classes starting that September. So my only remaining decision was what to do with the roughly three months in between.

Danny decided to go into business as an over-the-road tractor trailer owner-operator. You could make a really good living doing this. And Danny didn't seem to mind the thought of being on the road and away from home for a week or more at a time.

Over that summer, he started working on obtaining his commercial driver's license, or CDL for short. This was required to operate the big rigs. He already had driving experience working at our old company, so he was off to a good start. That and his extended family came together to finance the $50,000 that he needed to get started by buying a new truck.

Danny and I were out having lunch one day and catching up, when he mentioned that his father had just gotten him a summer temp job at the Garden State Arts Center[2]. Danny's father, Mike, was in a senior management position there. I had attended a concert at the Arts Center in 1973 as their guest, right after I helped Danny get his new job at my company. They gave me the full VIP treatment that night, as thanks for helping Danny.

---

2 The Garden State Arts Center (now the PNC Bank Arts Center) is an amphitheater in Holmdel, New Jersey. About 17,500 people can occupy the venue; there are 7,000 seats and the grass area can hold an additional 10,500 people. Concerts run from June through September, with events of many different types. It is ranked among the top five most successful amphitheaters in the country.

The complex was only about five years old at the time, and I thought it was very impressive. When Danny mentioned that his father could probably get me in there, too, if I wanted, it took me all of two seconds to decide. Absolutely!

The following Monday we both reported for work there. The hours were an adjustment for us. We were used to a 6 AM to 3 PM workday. This was more like 2 PM to 10 PM, or so. I had nothing going on in my life socially, so this was no problem. And Danny used the mornings to work on his CDL.

I approached this job with a fresh attitude, testing out an idea that I had been thinking about. I walked in on the first day feeling confident and not worrying about a damn thing … just be myself, and don't worry about everything. "Acting as-if," I called it. Act as if I had been there for years, and nothing could phase me.

Being more of a worrier myself, this was a stretch for me, but the Arts Center job was the perfect opportunity to try it out. I knew that I was leaving in about 12 weeks anyway, so what's the harm?

Within a few weeks, I quickly mastered the most basic skills needed to keep the stage working smoothly. And besides the wages, there was the additional bonus of hearing (and seeing a little, while working) a lot of great performances during the time that I was there. The 1975 season was a very good one:

Johnny Cash, Gordon Lightfoot, The Bee-Gees, James Taylor, Rich Little, Olivia Newton-John, Judy Collins, The Carpenters, Henry Mancini, Bob Hope, and Linda Ronstadt. I even caught the first day of Frank Sinatra's show, before I left the job.

Mixed in between these performances were things like the Bolshoi Ballet, Steve Lawrence and Eydie Gorme, and the Pittsburgh Symphony. Something for everyone.

But my story with Karen began one warm summer day in August of 1975.

# Monday, August 4, 1975

Whenever a new group arrives at the Arts Center, the first day is pretty chaotic. Sometimes the second day, too, with additional changes to fix newly discovered problems. There are van loads of equipment and wardrobe that need to hustled in and out of place. Then, on the stage, final placements, sound checks, adding or moving microphones, lighting adjustments, etc.

And so it was that day. The Carpenters were here.

Aside from doing everything required to get these activities done, it was just as important to be close by in case there was an immediate need for something unexpected. That need could be lending a hand helping to move some shipping cases, or as simple as making a drink run. There were no jobs on the stage that were not our responsibility. Ultimately, the success of the artist was the success of the Arts Center. That's how I viewed it, anyway.

In most respects, the Carpenters were no different than any other new group we hosted. They arrived well before noon, and there were already staff members here to help.

I arrived a bit after noon that Monday, as was my usual custom. Although there were timecards for everyone, I was a bit lax about the whole process. It's not that I refused to do it or anything. Absolutely not! But I normally just punched in when I arrived, and this may or may not be several hours before my normal scheduled start time. It was only because I would invariably forget to do so by 1:59, for my formal 2 PM start, because I was already busy doing something, and I'd just lost track of the time.

By the end of the week, my timecard looked more like a scratchpad at a bowling alley once my boss, Mike Betts, adjusted each day to the actual paid hours worked and made notes on it for the front office.

I was sorry to cause him additional work fixing all this, but short of skipping my timecard completely, this seemed the next best solution. It was probably only because of my years-long relationship with Mike that I was ever allowed to get away with this. Anyone else would probably have been told to shape up, or leave.

By about 3 PM, things seemed to be under control on stage. Three of us from the stage crew were still keeping busy, but mostly just standing by to be available. Richard Carpenter was at the piano going through some paperwork to prepare for that night's show. His sister Karen Carpenter was there, too, sitting in a folding chair just off to one side, almost hidden behind the piano.

You could be excused for not even knowing that she was there, because she was wearing a floppy hat that was hiding her face, and she was looking down reading something. Her pre-show work was done as well, so she was just hanging out.

Every now and then higher ups from the front office would come down to say hello, take some photos of themselves with the stars, gather autographs, etc. Karen stayed busy for five to ten minutes at a time with this, but the rest of the time she was just relaxing between those visits.

As usual, my good friend Danny was right up there in the middle of things on stage. I was amazed by just how quickly he blended into every new visiting group, as though he actually came here with *them*! I wish I could do that.

It was about this point that I thought I heard my name being mentioned in his discussion with Richard Carpenter. Yup … looks like he was doing a variation of his usual routine. Not to try and win money this time, but more to look good by association, perhaps? I could tell that a music memory game was coming.

Sure enough, a few minutes later I heard Danny say, "John, get your butt over here."

I walked up to the piano, and Danny introduced me to Richard. I was on the far side of the piano, so no handshakes, just hellos and head nods.

Danny started, "I was just telling Richard about your ability to identify songs with just one note. He seemed a little skeptical, so I thought that we should show him."

Notice the "we"!

"Sure thing," I said.

"Now?" Richard asked.

"Yes, whenever you're ready," I replied.

Richard played the chord of E flat on his piano.

After a second I replied: "'Bridge over Troubled Water,' Simon and Garfunkel."

Richard looked a bit surprised, because he then in fact played the first verse of that song.

Richard played the chord of C for the next song.

I replied: "'Imagine,' John Lennon."

Richard then played the first verse of "Imagine." He didn't seem as surprised this time, but I think he was trying harder to come up with a more challenging song.

Richard played the chord of B flat for the third song.

I was puzzled. Richard had stumped me, he thought.

"Can you give me just two or three more?" I asked, a bit curious myself as to what had just happened.

He did, playing me four notes, starting again from the beginning.

I replied, "'Get Together,' Youngbloods."

"I'm sorry," I added just then, "but Danny and I both forgot to mention the one and only rule of the game. We usually don't have to bring it up, because we're listening to the original songs on the radio, not played live. But the note has to be played on the same instrument that plays it in the recording for me to name it with just one note. That last one was supposed to be played on a guitar, not a piano, so that's why I needed a few more."

I could see that Richard was thinking about which one to try next when my friend Danny piped in, "He can do it with movies and TV shows, too. Ask him a trivia question," Danny said.

Richard looked like he was trying to switch mental gears just then to do a trivia question instead when we suddenly heard a voice from off to the side. It was Karen Carpenter. I had almost forgotten that she was still there on stage. But she had been sitting there quietly all along, just listening to our conversation.

"I have one for you," she said.

I turned to face her way and smiled. "Yes?" I said.

"Do you know the TV show 'Gilligan's Island[3]'?" she asked.

"Oh, sure," I said.

"What was the name of the musical group that visited the island in one episode?" she asked.

"That would be 'The Mosquitoes'," I replied.

"That's right!" Karen said. "Ok, now for the bonus round. What were the names of the band members?"

"Bingo, Bango, Bongo, and Irving," I said. "Irving was the drummer."

Karen had a huge grin on her face. "Yes, that's right! Wow!" she said. "That's amazing!"

---

[3] A popular TV comedy series in the 1960s about seven people stranded on an island in the Pacific Ocean.

I just smiled a thank you and said, "Well don't forget that you knew it, too. So that must mean you're kinda amazing yourself, right?"

Karen just had a sheepish grin on her face after I said that.

Just as I finished speaking, I happened to glance over toward Danny for a second. He was grinning from ear to ear at me. He was so proud. Not about the memory test — that was pretty much a given. But after all of his efforts, I had finally learned how to say more than two words to a girl, er … "woman."

By this point I could see that Richard was already standing, so I figured that we were through. Ok, break over, back to work. But for the rest of our time together on stage, I caught myself stealing a glimpse of Karen every now and then out of the corner of my eye.

It was actually a relief when she and Richard finally left the stage about an hour later to head for the dressing room. All I needed was for Karen to catch me looking at her more than one time and for her to get annoyed. But even after she left, I found myself daydreaming about her for the rest of the afternoon.

I'd always had a "thing" for Karen ever since the first time I saw her on TV back in 1970. And who could blame me? She was like the girl next door, plus beautiful and talented to boot. In thinking about it, she really was my first serious crush as a young adult. I had actually forgotten about all this, being bombarded with so many new experiences growing up.

But now she was front and center in my mind again. Now that I had actually talked to her, I seemed to automatically pick up where all those old forgotten thoughts had left off.

And I had to admit that she was *so* much better in person than I even imagined.

Soon enough the audience was there, and the night's show started. I was keeping busy, but I did look up now and then as time allowed, as I did with all the performances that summer.

This was also much easier for me to do now that she was focused on the audience and not on the fellow working in the shadows off to the side of the stage. And I enjoyed listening to their show, too. They had so many hit songs to perform.

After the show was over for the night, I hit the locker room to freshen up a bit and then walked out back to the employee parking area to get my bike and head home. It was actually a bit cool that evening for August. I was glad to have my leather jacket to retain my body heat, but I was wishing that I hadn't left my gloves at home that morning.

# Tuesday, August 5, 1975

The workday started a little early for me today. With a clear sky and a welcome break in the New Jersey humidity, I donned my helmet and riding gear to head out toward the Arts Center. This time I grabbed my gloves as well, having learned my lesson the previous night. There was nothing much going on at home, so I thought I'd get a jump on the day. And Lord knows that there is always something to do at work.

I rolled into the employee parking area a little before noon, even earlier than my normal early arrival. I stowed my riding gear in my locker, and then did a quick check in the mirror and combed away the damage that my helmet had done to my hair. After I punched in on the time clock I headed out toward the stage area to see who was around.

I wasn't 50 feet out of the door before my boss Mike came walking by in his usual brisk manner, and seeing me there, did a double take and altered his course toward me.

"Ah, you're here early today," he said. "Good boy. Before you do anything else, can you do me a favor and straighten out the gear near the south side of the stage? It was left a mess last night after the show, and I'll not be starting a new day with it still looking like that."

"Of course," I said with a nod. "I'll get right on it."

The south end of the stage is where all the massive sound equipment is tied into the performance area. Every microphone and instrument wire eventually made its way over here. There were probably twice as many total lines as were needed for a typical show. But no matter how many we used, they were each carefully labeled and ready to go live with just the flick of a switch on the master console.

But with miles and miles of wire came miles and miles of mess. So, much like a fireman maintains his hoses, these cables needed to be neatly stowed, too, for rapid deployment.

I hadn't worked this side of the stage the previous night, so I didn't see any of this before I left. It wasn't really *that* bad, just not quite ready for any type of inspection. But this was Mike.

It felt longer just because it was boring work, but after about an hour I finally started to make a major dent in the mess. I was probably doing more than was needed, but starting with perfection on a Monday actually got us through the workweek much better. But no one had done that yesterday, so this was more like Tuesday catchup.

During the time that most artists are here, relatively few changes were needed to the sound equipment after the second or *maybe* third day.

While I was sorting out the wires, out of the corner of my eye I could see constant activity on the stage just above me. The main curtain was open, so I could see everything, including backstage. Slowly at first, but over time, more and more people were starting to drift in. But it was a very casual thing, with no large groups or loud conversations to snap me back to reality, just people milling about, doing what they needed to do, just as I was.

I could usually tune all these activities out, much like someone talking to a friend can tune out the background noises of the bar where they're meeting over drinks.

It was about this time that I half noticed a figure working their way across the stage. They moved quietly yet deliberately, so much so that they were only a few feet away before I realized that this person was actually headed straight toward me. But it wasn't Mike this time, coming to inspect his precious wires. When I finally looked up to see who it was, I saw that it was Karen Carpenter.

"Hey, there, Mr. One Note. Remember me?" she said with a grin, as she plopped herself down at the edge of the stage, her legs dangling over the side.

I confess that my heart probably skipped *more* than just one beat when I realized who it was. Wow! Karen Carpenter. And she was talking to *me*.

"Yes, *yes*. You're that drummer girl. Right? You know, the one in the band?" I said with a feigned look of uncertainty on my face. But my grin surely gave away my ruse.

"Yes, that's right," she said, playing along. "That's me. I also get up and sing now and then. You know, to kill time."

Both smiling, we held each other's gaze for another second, secretly betting, it seems, on who would break character first. In the end we both let out a small chuckle at the same time, almost as if on cue.

"Yes, I caught the 'singing' part of your show last night," I said. "It was great!"

"Thank you," she said, in an almost practiced way. Not dismissive at all, but more like a reflex action, probably from having said it a million times before in the last few years.

She was still smiling politely, though, so I continued, "I have to say, you've really got your stage presence down to a science now. I loved the way you worked the crowd last night. Oh, and that extended drum solo near the end of the show, wow! You really do great ghost notes[4]."

From the look on her face I could tell that she was a bit taken aback by what I had just said, but not in a bad way. It was more like the surprise of hearing someone who is clearly not Asian start speaking perfect Japanese.

"What do you know from ghost notes?" she said, slightly confused.

"Oh, I know a little bit about a lot of things I guess ... just enough to be dangerous," I replied. "But I really love music."

"Well, thanks. Thank you," she said, regarding the ghost notes compliment. As she regained her composure, she seemed to be looking at me in a new light.

"Sorry. I guess I'm not used to talking to civilians about drumming stuff. You know, people who aren't musicians," she said.

A smile slowly returned to her face. A bit bigger perhaps this time around, than it was before? I was glad. I was worried

---

[4] A ghost note on drums is a soft and barely audible note played between two louder, more prominent notes.

for a second that I had crossed some type of line by commenting too much about her performance.

"So what did you mean when you said that my stage presence seemed better? Have you seen us before, in person I mean?" she asked.

This wasn't just someone fishing around for a compliment. She really wanted to know.

"I have actually, yes," I said. "Back in 1973. Right here at the Arts Center. It was your very first night here."

"Oh, you were there!" she exclaimed. "Wow! Yes I remember that night. Man, I was really stressed out during that show. It was our first time here, and things were *not* going smoothly at all, both on the stage and off. I kinda felt like we needed to refund everyone's money on that one," she quipped. "It was a disaster."

"Oh, not at all," I said in my most reassuring voice. "You guys were terrific. If you were having problems that night, it sure didn't show."

I held my gaze and my simple smile a bit longer this time, sensing that she really was serious about her unease over that performance, even though it was over two years ago. Karen truly was a perfectionist.

"So," she said, "were you working the stage back then, too? Did I miss you that night?"

"No, not that time," I said. "I was here strictly as a civilian. You know, just for fun."

Karen smiled at the reuse of her own word.

"Yes," she said, getting back to the stage presence question. "Terry has been helping me a lot with my performance. Terry Ellis, I mean, my boyfriend. I've really learned how to be comfortable up on stage," she paused. "Well, better anyway."

"Oh … Great … I mean it really shows," I added with a nod.

At that moment I felt like a pin had pricked me, and all the air inside was slowly leaking out. "Her boyfriend." I had to quickly regain my composure before she made any connection and judged me to be the silly fool that I probably was. So I fell back on the tried and true tactic of distraction. Well, an attempt at distraction anyway.

"You know I actually met you and Richard that night, after the show. You were signing autographs, and I got both of you to sign my program," I said.

I paused for a second, losing my train of thought under the pressure of this crazy moment.

"I still have it," I added.

I realized right away that I was starting to sound too much like a nerdy fan. My idea wasn't working at all.

"Oh, yes, we try to do that every time, whenever we can. It's important," she said, her voice and gaze trailing off ever so slightly it seemed.

I felt like the conversation was starting to lag. Had she really sensed my discomfort with that boyfriend thing after all, and was she falling back into reflex-answer mode, all while quietly eyeing the exits? John, you idiot!

Out of desperation, I quickly added without much thought, "You probably don't remember this, but after you signed the program for me, I thanked you doing my very best Donald Duck impersonation."

Karen's eyes flashed wide open, unblinking, and I wondered for a second what I had done. Did that come out wrong or something?

"That was *you*!" she half shouted. "You son of a bitch! I almost peed in my pants when you did that! I laughed so hard that I had tears in my eyes!"

Yikes! Talk about a rollercoaster of emotions. Here I was, going for a cheap laugh to try and save my keister. And then I'm thinking, "She's going to punch me in the nose!" But in the end it was all good, thank God.

"*Why*, for heavens sake, did you do that?" she said.

I looked at her in a rather embarrassed fashion and confessed, "I really just wanted you to smile at me, that's all. And I knew you liked Disney kinda stuff. But I'm *really* sorry if I pissed you off. I sure didn't expect that *that* was going to be your reaction."

Karen looked at me and gave me a smile, half shaking her head from side to side, and said, "I wasn't pissed at you, man. You know what I was just saying about being really stressed that day? The performance? All the problems? Well by the end of the night I was wound up so tight that I was ready to explode. I felt like I could barely sign my name for the autographs. Your DD impression[5] was the last straw, but in a good way I suppose. It was so silly that it was perfect. All that stress and emotion came gushing out, right then and there! God, I felt so much better. But by the time I found some tissues to dry my eyes, you were gone. Richard and everyone else were all still staring at me. They didn't hear what you had said, and they couldn't figure out why on earth I had suddenly turned into a crazy person!"

"I remember," I said. "Everyone was looking at you, and then looking at me like, 'What the *hell* did you *do* to her?' I thought I'd better split while I still could."

Wow! What a recovery! After my own stupid insecurities. I felt like I had once again gone from zero to hero in Karen's eyes. Twice in two days! What was happening to me?

But just as I was almost starting to savor the moment, I became aware of an eerie quiet on the stage. When I risked a look around, I saw that all eyes were on us. Or I should say, on Karen. Her reaction this time had drawn just as much attention as it had two years ago, except that *this* time there was no place for me to run and hide. This time was going to be different, for *me*.

From behind my back I could feel the warm breath on my neck of a familiar voice.

"Is this fellow bothering you, Miss?"

It was Mike Betts, my boss. He had heard all the commotion and had zoomed in on me and Karen as being the source,

---

5 Karen loved to make up nicknames and abbreviations.

along with everyone else watching from around the stage it seems, because all activity had come to a complete standstill.

Mike was smiling politely, but his question was deadly serious.

As a rule, we were not allowed to fraternize with "the talent." After all, these people were here for a job, and they were pestered enough in their lives. All of us working the stage were supposed to be professionals. For us, it was strictly a case of "speak only when you are spoken to."

Not getting an answer as quickly as he expected, and by now sensing that there might be a *real* problem afoot, Mike quietly asked once again, "Is everything ok, Miss?"

Karen, the consummate comedian, sensed the irony of the moment, so she took a long second to reply. With a most devious gleam in her eye and a smile on her lips, all of which I could plainly see but Mike could not, she slowly eyed me up and down, almost as if she were looking at me for the first time, but over the top of some imaginary pair of horn-rimmed eyeglasses.

"This fellow?" she asked innocently, "Why, no, he's not bothering me at all. We're just having a good laugh together, that's all. Isn't that right, John?"

It suddenly hit me that this was the first time she had ever spoken my name, and the thought of it seemed to make my heart stop. But at the same time it was a strangely warm feeling.

Until this point, I wasn't even sure whether she knew my name or not. I was probably just "the Gilligan's Island' guy" in her mind.

All this time, Karen's eyes were locked onto me, looking for my reaction. Wondering … would it be one of panic? Fear? What would he do under the spotlight? She was clearly enjoying the moment.

"Yes," I said, recovering quickly. "Karen and I are old friends. We go back years."

Karen smiled as I said this, picking up on the reference to our 1973 "meeting."

"That's right," she said, finally half turning toward Mike to reassure him with her smile. "Thanks for asking, but everything is justtt fineee."

"I'm glad to hear that," Mike said. Then, as he began to turn to leave, he abruptly stopped … "Oh, I almost forgot why I came out here. Can you stop by my office to see me 'when you're done here'," he said to me.

As he said this, Mike's eyes shifted for an instant from me over to Karen, and then back to me again.

"Of, course, boss. I'll be right over. You bet," I said bashfully. I had a strong feeling that he wasn't talking about being done organizing the wires!

Karen and I both watched silently for a moment as Mike walked away. The rest of the small crowd started to disperse as well. Show's over folks.

When Mike finally turned the corner and was out of sight, Karen clasped both of her hands over her mouth and she burst out laughing. "Oh, my God, John! I'm so sorry!" she said. "I sure didn't mean to get you in trouble!"

There it was again: my name!

"Whew! That was a close one," I said. "Do you realize that you could have had me fired with just a frown on your forehead?" I teased, as I stuck my hand between the buttons on my shirt, and pretended that my heart was beating out of my chest. I quickly smiled and added, "I'm kidding. Don't worry about it, I'll be fine. Besides, it's good payback for two years ago, don't you think?"

Karen had a huge grin over the thought of that one!

What she didn't appreciate was that she was the single best "get out of jail free" pass that anyone at the Arts Center could ever hope for. As long as she wasn't really upset, I had no reason to worry.

After a few second's pause, Karen looked back over toward me and asked, "So how do you like working here? Are they treating you well?"

I kinda nodded and said, "It's really a dream job. You get paid to stand around and hang out with celebrities, lots of free shows and plenty of fresh air and sunshine. When it's not raining, I mean."

Karen was smiling but sensing the sarcasm in my words.

"No, I'm kidding. It's really great, but actually it's only a temporary thing, just for the summer," I said. "I'm starting school in September. Danny and I used to work together at another place. We were both laid off. His father is Mike Betts, who you just met."

Karen grinned.

"Mike got Danny and me in here to help out for the summer. Mike is great, sort of a second father to me. It's temporary for Danny too. He's working on plans for his own business," I said.

"Temporary lives, huh? Yeah, I know about that," Karen said.

After a few seconds Karen asked, "Is Danny the guy from yesterday, with the music quiz?"

"Oh, I'm sorry, I didn't think to explain," I said. "But yes, that's him. He's my best friend."

"Mr. Casanova is your best friend?" she replied.

"Oh, no. He didn't hit on you or something, did he?" I asked. "Because I'll punch him for you if you want me to. I'm serious," I said with a grin, but trying to do some damage control with a joke, just in case.

"No, not really. He introduced himself right away, though. But you can always tell when a guy is trying hard to get you to 'like' him," she said.

"That's Danny. He can talk his way into a house of ill repute and find a way to get a free one," I said.

"Geez," I thought, "Probably not the best analogy."

Karen seemed to get a kick out of it, though. "Yeah, after talking to him yesterday, I can see that happening!" she said.

After a moment's pause, she said, "Well, I should probably get going. I have tonight to get ready for, and I'm sure that Rich is wondering where the hell I am. This is only our second day here, so we're still getting settled in with things. Still lots to do. But I sure have enjoyed our talk," she said with a wink.

"Oh, me too, thanks!" I blurted out, wishing that it was something more clever.

Karen got a few steps away, paused for a second, and then turned back around, as though she *too* had forgotten why she came out here. "By the way, I wanted to thank you for talking to me," she said.

I was clearly confused by that one, and I started to speak, "But you just ..."

Karen cut me off, anticipating my question. "No, I wanted to thank you for talking to *me*. Not Karen Carpenter the singer, but *me*."

After a second, she continued, "Sometimes people seem to forget that deep down I'm just a person, too. Every time we go somewhere new, people walk around on eggshells for days, like they're terrified of me or something. By the time they figure out that I don't usually bite, we're moving on to the next show, and it starts all over again. I hate it. I mean, I suppose I understand why. But ... So thank you for talking to *me*."

I couldn't think of anything to say, but I expect that the ear-to-ear grin still stuck on my face said it all. But I nodded my acknowledgement nonetheless.

"Catch you tomorrow!" she said, as she slowly backed away.

With that, Karen turned around and she was gone, and I resigned myself to getting back to work and finishing up these damn cables. Suddenly my job seemed very dull.

Honestly, my brain was spinning a hundred miles an hour all that day and the rest of the evening. I was replaying that 15-minute conversation over and over in my mind, word for word, burning it all into my memory.

I was actually slightly embarrassed when I finally remembered my promise to go see Mike in his office in the middle of all this. It was an hour or more later than I expected.

I got to his open door and said, "Knock, knock," to get his attention.

He looked up from his papers and motioned for me to take a seat. He was smiling again, and I was relieved to see that. Perhaps I had stayed away just long enough for him to cool off!

"John, I need to ask a favor. A big one, though. I just learned that on Thursday morning we're getting a special truck in here with some sound equipment that we've been waiting for since May. It's going to be here early, around 7:30 AM, and I need a few trustworthy people to come in and help with the installation. You'll be working directly with the sound engineers on this. They'll be in charge of the actual install. You'll just be there to assist them.

"It won't be dirty work, just a lot of wiring, so street clothes are fine. But you can bring a change of clothes along if you want to, in case it's a hot one that day. I can't risk bringing any knuckleheads in on this one. It's going to be a hand-picked crew. We need to be 100% up and running for Thursday night's show. I'm sure that your girlfriend, Karen, will appreciate that we get it all working right for her, don't you think?" he said with a wink and a smile.

I smiled and nodded back.

"You and Danny would be here from the stage team. Can you do it?" he said.

After the crazy day that I'd already had, I felt a bit like a punch-drunk boxer who couldn't take anymore. All this info was spinning around in my head, but I somehow found myself nodding in agreement before it even had a chance to all sink in. It was obviously the answer that Mike was counting on.

"Thank you, son, that's a load off my mind. I know it's short notice, and I know it means coming in early and facing a 16-hour day. But I take it as a personal favor," he said.

As I stood up I repeated in my head: "Ok, 7:30 AM, Thursday, got it," just to remember it. As I turned to leave I realized that Thursday was normally my day off! I mentioned this to Mike, and he said to consider it overtime if I wanted or, if I'd rather, just switch days off. I still wasn't thinking that clearly, so I just assured Mike that we'd figure it out one way or another afterward, and I left the office.

Other than the off season, there never really is a good time for new sound equipment installs, big ones anyway. The Arts Center was completely booked from June to September, ideally without a single day off. But this delivery was so late that the 1975 show season was almost two months under way. Oh, well, always something new!

The rest of the day was a blur of activity, but I can't really recall much of it in detail. There were a few funny looks and snide remarks thrown at me by a some members of the crew after the whole "Karen" thing, but no permanent damage. Word gets around quickly here. I never did see her again until her show started. She looked so good up there under the lights.

When Karen got to her drum solo near the end of the show, I could almost swear that she was looking around to see if I was watching and showing off those ghost notes for me! Talk about the wish making the thought. I never did manage to catch her eye that night, which is just as well. She had her job to do. But she really seemed to be playing with a new energy up there compared to the previous night.

I'm embarrassed to say that I don't really recall any of the ride home on my bike that night, which is a scary thought indeed. You really need to be focused when you're riding a motorcycle, especially in New Jersey. You're pretty much invisible to most car drivers. It was almost midnight when I finally hit the sheets. I think that I was asleep the instant my head hit the pillow. Sweet dreams indeed!

# Wednesday, August 6, 1975

For being so tired — not so much physically as mentally — it was a nasty surprise to find myself wide awake at 4 AM on Wednesday morning. Thank goodness I didn't need to be anywhere early. I turned off my alarm clock just in case I did manage to fall back asleep, because I sure didn't want anything to wake me up again if I did. But sleep was not in the cards for the moment.

I found myself replaying the events of the previous day. Not so much to memorize them anymore, but this time just to enjoy the memories.

For some reason my mind kept coming back around to Karen's comment about her boyfriend, and my own foolish reaction to it that I tried so desperately to hide. And it caught me off guard that it had all caught me so off guard. Does that sentence even make sense?

Why on earth should it bother me that she has a boyfriend? She's a person, too, just as she reminded me a few short hours ago. She deserves happiness and a good life. We all want that.

And I sure don't know her at all, not really, I mean. And Lord knows that she barely knows me. If anything, I might come to her mind the next time she sees a Donald Duck cartoon, or "Gilligan's Island," perhaps? How's that for your ego John!

So what is it then about celebrity that makes us feel that somehow these people are ours? Why was I a tinge jealous?

Thinking back, I remembered reading about the Beatles and how, when Paul McCartney was first married, some female fans got hysterically upset. Somehow Paul was no longer *available* to them, as if he ever really was.

But is it as simple as this?

Deep down, do we all really know that nothing can *ever* happen — we will never meet these famous people; they will never fall in love with us — but *deep down* we still prefer to cling to the dream that somehow all these things *could* happen?

In our minds, do these people become ours simply because we've built an entire imaginary world around them? We've devoted dozens (or hundreds?) of hours of our *own* lives just in thinking about them. Dreaming — no, *knowing* — how perfect it would all be if only they were in our lives.

After spending all this time, and thought, and energy on them, how could they *not* be ours? They are the center of our dream world, after all. We certainly wouldn't do this for a *stranger*, would we? That would just be… crazy, wouldn't it?

Is this the unconscious thought process that all fans go through to one degree or another? I was starting to wonder.

And then — *then*, after all this — some inconvenient detail emerges that snaps us back to harsh reality and the simple truth that all of these dreams are in fact an illusion, which, by definition, can't ever be real.

It's also strange how the simplest of things can so easily topple our whole imaginary world, even worlds that we truly didn't appreciate existed. Even just a single word. A word like "boyfriend."

Are we living real lives here, or are we all just living a fantasy?

And what of all those people who firmly believe that if they could *only* meet their idols, everything would be ok. That person would instantly *know* I was the one for them. Are these the same folks who are so in awe that they become completely tongue-tied if that moment of contact ever does come around?

How sad is all this? And how sad am I, because I now find myself in this exact same situation.

Karen Carpenter is a goddess to me, and she has the voice of an angel. When she was singing "Close to You" on the Ed Sullivan show for the first time — in that cute outfit, with her long hair and bangs framing that beautiful face — she was singing to me. The rest of the world may have been watching, but she was *singing* just for me.

No doubt a thousand other guys all share this same belief.

But now, just yesterday, I had to pinch myself to think that I was actually hanging out with her. Me, a blue-collar kid from Linden. I was talking to her. She was talking to me. I was listening to her, but more importantly, *she* was listening to *me*!

How I found the strength of will to talk to her at all, I'll never know. I liken it to a tight-rope walker: You just have to *do* it.

You don't *think* about it, and for heaven's sake you don't look down. You just *do* it or you never will.

Talking to anyone else isn't a problem, Right? So why should this be?

But to be honest, it was so natural talking to her that none of this even came to mind at the time. If anything, I may have been too flip with her!

And yet somehow my own situation seems entirely worse precisely because I *have* met my dream girl, and I *did* talk to her, and somehow I didn't panic and instantly destroy my own dream in the process. But this was pure luck on my part, not any skill.

And now my entire future seems to rest on a knife edge. The door is cracked open for me with Karen, but for what, I have no idea. But any *one* thing that I do or say from now on could decide the fate of all my dreams.

Wow … I'm starting to understand why all those fans got tongue-tied. Did I just screw with my own head or what? What will happen from now on when I see her? Will I become a drooling vegetable? Why do I do these things! Talk about putting a whammy on yourself …

I don't know what time it was when I finally did fall back asleep. And Lord knows that I didn't come up with any more answers to all these questions while I tossed and turned. All I knew for sure was that I couldn't wait to see Karen again if I could.

It was almost 10 AM when I did finally wake up. I got my eight hours of sleep, eventually, even if it was just four hours, times twice. After a long shower and a quick breakfast, I thought I *might* just head over to the Arts Center a little early today.

So why was I suddenly getting butterflies in my stomach, just at the thought of being there?

My Harley was running strong as I rode to work. One of the hidden benefits of riding a bike is that whatever problems you have on your mind, a good ride will usually blow them all out of your head. Such was the case today.

It would be the end of the summer before the Garden State Parkway would finally lift its ban on motorcycles, so for now I had to make my way to the Arts Center via the back roads, as usual. A pity because the Arts Center is a prominent feature *on* the Parkway! But even taking the back way, with all the traffic lights, I still arrived in good spirits and feeling like maybe I had a clear handle on things.

And as it turned out, it would take all of about 10 minutes to prove me wrong …

No sooner had I turned off my bike and stepped off when I heard a familiar voice from over near the gatehouse.

"Mike wants to see you in his office as soon as you get in." It was my buddy Wayne Kowal, one of the uniformed security people for the site.

Wayne has been with the Arts Center since it opened about seven years back, and he knew pretty much every one and every thing around here. If my boss, Mike, wasn't around to ask something, I'd probably ask Wayne for his opinion first over a dozen other people on site. I liked Wayne.

Normally I could tell if he was nearby, even 50 feet away, because you can always smell his cigar long before you can see him. But on days like this when the wind was coming from the wrong direction he could surprise you.

I walked over to the gatehouse where he was standing just inside the doorway. Before I could even say anything, I heard him say, "You look a little tired this morning, John. Rough night?"

"A little," I said. "I guess I didn't get a good night's sleep."

"Oh? What was her name?" he said with a wink.

Did I forget to mention that Wayne is also my connection for any hot gossip around the site?

"In the first dream I had, or the second?" I asked with a smile.

"Ah, you're no fun ..." he grumbled.

I only fed Wayne site news, but nothing about people gossip — you know, who's dating who, affairs, breakups, that kind of stuff. Not that I was in the loop for most of those things anyway. That was usually front office stuff. The stage crew were all still guys back then. But Wayne never stopped pumping people for information. And sooner or later, he knew everything that was going on.

"I'd better go and see what I screwed up ... er, what Mike wants, I mean," I said with a smile.

Wayne gave me a grin and a dismissive wave of his arm, like a cop directing traffic. "Get out of here," he said with a laugh.

After a quick stop at my locker, I was off to Mike's office.

"You wanted to see me, boss?" I asked when I got there.

Mike was shuffling through some clipboards and papers (this being the pre-computer days) and he didn't even look up, he just said, "Yes."

Gee … maybe I was right about the screwup thing after all?

He finally found the light blue slip of paper that he was looking for and handed it to me. Still barely looking up, he said, "When you're done with this, report back here for your regular duties."

"Ok," I said. After a second I added, "Is there anything that I need to bring?" Which was my backhanded way of fishing around for a clue as to what this was all about.

After a moments pause he said, "Just yourself," in a rather dismissive fashion. "Better hurry," he added.

Mike was really acting strangely and he was still barely looking at me. I was quickly glancing over the note while still at the door, just in case I had a question, when Mike looked up briefly and we made eye contact.

He guessed my wonder about the mystery note, but before I could even open my mouth to speak, he just shrugged his shoulders and said, "I dunno … ," and then went back to his papers.

The preprinted form didn't have many blocks filled out: just my name penciled in, also the building and room info, and ASAP in the time box. That was it. So I headed over to building "A," on the other side of the campus.

I hadn't been there all that many times — one or two meetings, and a few birthday parties — so I had to follow the wall maps to find the right room.

After a few minutes I turned a corner and found it. Room 127? Check. The door was closed, so I knocked and let myself in. I immediately panicked and did a double take of the slip of paper when I got inside, because who was sitting there at the table but Karen Carpenter.

She looked up from her magazine and said, "Hi, again!"

Oh geezs. This is embarrassing. Of all the wrong rooms to walk into. She's gonna think I'm stalking her or something. All because of some sloppy handwriting!

"Oh, excuse me!" I said, as I started backing out the door just as quickly as I came in, all while checking the slip to see if it was really room 121 that I wanted and not room 127.

"No, no, no. You're in the right place," she said. "Come on in."

I was a bit flustered, for sure. What was going on? And after all the head-spinning thoughts of last night, my confidence level sure wasn't what I needed it to be right now.

Karen sensed my continued hesitation.

"Come, sit. Can I get you a drink?" she asked, motioning me toward the chair next to hers.

My throat *was* a bit parched at the moment … Wayyy too many surprises for one morning.

"Whatever you're having will be fine, thanks. Don't go to any trouble," I said.

"It's iced tea. It's just from a can though. Is that ok?" she replied.

"Yes, thanks," I said.

Karen set my drink down in front of me, and then sat down herself. A few seconds later, she started, "I ran into your friend Mike Betts in the parking lot this morning when I came in. I wasn't sure of the exact protocol here, but I asked him if I could have someone from the site to assist me this afternoon, and he suggested you."

"He did?" I said. I had to catch myself because I blurted it out more like a surprise than a question.

"Well, yes …" she hesitated, looking down at the table for a second, and then back up at me, "after I said 'anyone else?' to the first two people he named."

With that she broke out into an embarrassed grin, having been found out.

Before I could even react to all this, she said, "I'm sorry, John, but as far as I can tell, you're either the only person here with a brain in his head or you're the only one that I've

51

met who isn't terrified to be around me! So you were the one I asked for."

Wow! So much to take in. Thankfully I was quick on my feet, despite my bad night's sleep.

"Well, those two things are *not* mutually exclusive around here, but I hear what you're saying," I said with a smile.

Karen smiled back.

"Mike was probably suggesting one of the regular liaison guys that we have who take care of our visiting artists," I added.

"I'm sure," she said, "but we already have one of those. I think he runs the other way anytime he sees me."

"That's probably the new guy, Tom Adler," I thought to myself. If I was a betting man, I'd say that he'll be gone before the end of the month, especially if he's scared of Karen. They probably gave Karen to him to break him in. Karen is a pussycat.

You have to be a real people person to be a liaison. I couldn't do it myself. Wouldn't want to. Oh sure, when you're working with Karen Carpenter most everyone (except Tom?) wants the job. But many of the acts in here are self-centered egotists and a general pain in the butt. Sometimes it seems as though they torture our liaisons just for fun.

"So you just need me to help with things that your liaison should be doing?" I asked. "If you had one that you could find?"

I wasn't actually even sure what those duties were on a daily basis, but I thought I could figure it out if I had to. I'm not afraid to ask for help.

"Not exactly," Karen said. "Let me be straight with you. I *really* enjoyed our talk yesterday. I didn't even realize how much until late last night. When I couldn't sleep, I started thinking about the previous day. I really do my clearest thinking at four in the morning. I realized that I've been in a slow funk for a while now. Way too many days on the road and no one to really talk to outside my own little circle within the group. We've all heard each other's stories and each other's complaints so many times that we often just sit there in silence when we have some unexpected time off, especially toward the end of the tour. And that's ok … life on the road and all that. Also one of the many reasons why we can't wait to get back home.

"But what I also realized this morning was that I really had my batteries recharged yesterday, and I think it was because I ran into you and we talked and had a few laughs together. You're the first one in ages who has treated me like a person and not an object from day one. I think I just need that human connection with someone I can relate to. Like a best friend or something, but someone who knew me before I was famous and who isn't intimidated by me. But you've *never* been intimidated by me. That's what makes the difference. So that's the reason I asked Mike for you," she said.

Wow! I loved her honesty. It really took my breath away.

"Karen, I absolutely enjoyed talking with you too. And, like you, I was up early this morning, with everything we talked about spinning around in my head. I was surprised, myself, in thinking about it, that I wasn't nervous at all talking to you. But it just felt natural. I actually started to wonder if I was being disrespectful by being so casual with you. All I know is, by the time I fell back asleep, I was really hoping that I'd see you again, and maybe we'd get another chance to talk."

Karen was beaming when I was done.

"Oh, I'm so glad! Sometimes I have a bit of a buster sense of humor, and some folks don't handle it well. Especially coming from Karen Carpenter, quote unquote. It's really a good thing though because it means I'm comfortable with you. But there were one or two times yesterday when I wished I could tell what you were thinking because I could see the gears spinning in your head, so I wasn't sure. But I'm glad that it wasn't because I was scaring you off," she said.

"Oh, not at all," I said. "It was fun! You were just keeping me on my toes is all. I enjoy the give and take. I was more worried that I was being too direct with *you*. I thought that you might not take it well, coming from a stranger — that and with you being a celebrity and all."

"But that's what I *crave*," she said. "I'm surrounded by people who are trying to second guess what I want to hear. Other than maybe Richard and my mom, everyone is too afraid to say no to me. But if *no* is the answer, then that's what I want to hear. I'm probably not explaining myself very well, but I hope you can understand."

"I really do. It all makes perfect sense. Say no more," I assured her.

But just then the reality of the whole situation kinda hit me. Were we just gonna sit here in this office and talk for the next few hours until her show? Boy, I'm not always a great one to come up with interesting topics under pressure. More times than not, interesting topics seem to find me. What did I just agree to? This might be awkward.

"So what did you want to talk about?" I asked, suddenly feeling very much on the spot.

"Well, I *did* have one thing that I'd like to ask you, if I may?" Karen said.

"Terrific," I thought. "Not awkward!"

"Of course," I said. "What's that?"

After a few seconds to collect her thoughts, Karen said, "What the *heck* did you tell your boss, Mike, about me!?"

Ouch … awkward.

I felt like I had just been sucker punched. Not that I thought she was trying to be mean or anything, but I had absolutely *no* idea what she was talking about.

"I have absolutely *no* idea what you are talking about," I said.

"Your boss, Mike? What did you say to him about me?" she repeated.

"I didn't say one word about you to Mike. Or to anyone else for that matter. Pinky swear," I said.

The pinky swear seemed to help a little, thank God.

"What happened with you and Mike to make you think that I had? I mean, what did he say to you?" I asked.

Karen started, "This morning ... when I was asking him for someone?"

"Yes?" I said.

"Well ... everything was fine, at first," she continued. "He said the first name. I passed. Everything was fine. He said the *second* name. I passed. Everything was fine. He said *your* name. I said ok. That's when it happened."

"What happened?" I said.

Karen paused for a second, not quite sure how to phrase it. "He started *grinning* at me!"

"Grinning?" I said. "You mean he laughed at you?" This didn't sound like Mike at all.

"No, not laughing — grinning, just like I said. He had this crazy shit-faced grin that wouldn't go away! At one point I actually checked my blouse because I wondered 'Am I exposing myself to this man or something and don't know it? What the heck is going on?' He just wouldn't stop grinning! I mean I was probably only there for a minute or two, but I think that if I didn't turn to leave, he'd still be out in the parking lot grinning!" she said.

Now the pieces were slowly falling into place.

"Wow, what a crazy way to start your day. I'm so sorry. I'm glad that at least you didn't cancel your request for me to be here because of it," I said.

"Ohhh, no. If we were only going to have one conversation today, I was going to make sure that I got to the bottom of this," she replied.

Karen wasn't angry. Actually, I don't think she was ever angry about any of it even in the morning. She just wanted to know.

I was really starting to like this girl.

"When Mike gave me the slip to come over here this morning, he was being very mysterious. I've known him for almost 10 years, and I've never seen him like this," I said.

But before I could continue, Karen cut in, "So you never told him we were sleeping together or anything like that?"

"Absolutely not! I was serious before, I never once mentioned your name to him," I said.

"So did he ever mention *my* name to you? Since yesterday, you know, by the stage where he saw us?" she asked.

"Well *yes* he did. It did come up once," I said.

"Go on," she added.

"Well, nothing important, really. We were talking about some new sound equipment being installed tomorrow, and he just commented that we had to have everything working 100% for your show," I said.

I said this last part with my fingers crossed a little bit, behind my back.

"So that's it? Nothing else?" she replied.

"Well, just as a joke I'm sure, he loves to bust chops. He did call you my girlfriend," I said.

"That's it?" Karen said again. "So what do you think is behind all this grinning stuff?"

"Well, I can only guess," I said, "but believe me, I intend to find out before this day is over. But if I had to *guess,* I'd say that it's only because he thinks I'm the luckiest SOB walking the planet because Karen Carpenter likes me."

And he'd be right too.

Now it was *my* turn to look at Karen in a whole new light. Wow, she was formidable. I had sensed that she was never actually angry about any of this, and I was right. How else could she have been so perky just a few minutes before while we were talking? She'd have to be one hell of an actress.

What I was seeing was never anger; it was determination. I could see how she had come so far so fast in her career — she was tough. I may owe Tom Adler, her liaison, an apology! Karen was no pussycat! Scratch that (no pun intended). When everything was going as it should, *then* Karen was a pussycat. But she is a perfectionist. And she expects nothing less from everyone else around her.

I was starting to appreciate poor Tom's predicament: new guy; screw up a few simple things; Karen. What a bad mix.

If anything, Tom's real mistake — the important one I mean — is that he has not yet learned how to recognize the difference between a strong woman and an angry one. Apples and oranges. But it's also a pretty common male problem, I'm sorry to say. No wonder Tom has been hiding.

It took just a nanosecond for all these thoughts to flash through my head, but in that same blink of an eye Karen's whole demeanor had changed. "My" Karen was back again.

"Thanks for being honest with me about all that," she said. "It means a lot to me. It doesn't happen often, but every now and then, especially in the tabloids, there is some hot gossip about me and someone else. Usually built on a thread of truth, like us talking by the stage yesterday, for example. But the rest is all fabricated. It's probably great for the ego of whoever it happens to be, 'so-and-so *made it* with Karen Carpenter.' I didn't think that you were that type, but I've been wrong about plenty of other stuff in the past, so ..."

"I'm not one to kiss and tell," I assured her.

Karen's eyes opened a bit wider at hearing that.

"You dummy," I thought to myself. "You really need to filter your thoughts a little better. No wonder you'd never make it as a liaison."

A second later, however, a smile returned to her face. "Good to know," she said with a chuckle.

She sat there looking at me for a moment and said, "You're funny. You never have been afraid of me for even one second, have you? Do you know how I can tell? Your eyes. I

59

was watching you yesterday while Mike was grilling you. When I first met you I wasn't sure if you were just putting on a brave act around me or if this was really you. But even with Mike getting in your face and you almost getting fired, you were fine. If anything, you seemed amused! That's when I knew."

She continued. "Most times I get one of three reactions from regular people: Terrified, Intimidated, or Goofy. The terrified run, the intimidated can't speak, and the goofy ones just grin. It's gotten to where I can usually tell who is who from 20 feet away, just by their initial reaction when they see me! The fans are usually the goofy ones, and that's fine. We get a kick out of their behavior sometimes."

She paused for a second, as though she had just thought of something.

"Come to think of it, that's one of the reasons why I always assumed I'd eventually settle down with someone else who is in the music or film business, because they understand all this. Or someone successful, but some of them can get goofy too!" she said. "It's not that I'm a snob or anything, but terrified, intimidated, or goofy is not my idea of a dating pool!"

"You know I saw you watching me while Mike was interrogating me. You looked like you were having a good old time! I just assumed it was because you had a hidden evil streak," I teased.

"See that right there? That's what I'm talking about. *No* one talks to me like that!" she said with a laugh.

"Whew!" I said. "I'm glad I was wrong about that evil streak."

Just then Karen got a dead serious look on her face.

"Did I *say* you were wrong?" she said, as she stared at me, unblinking.

After a few seconds passed, a huge grin started showing on her face.

"Spot test. See, you passed again," she said.

"Geez! Don't do that! Did you take acting classes in college or something?" I said with a smile.

Karen was laughing by now. "No! But I *was* being considered for a part in a John Wayne movie once. But I didn't get it," she said.

"Probably because they were looking for someone sweet and innocent ..." I mumbled under my breath, but loud enough for her to hear.

"What did you just say, Mister?" she asked.

"Hmm?" I replied. "Did you hear me say something?"

With that we both burst out laughing.

"You're a lot of fun Karen. But *maybe* we should go for a walk outside to talk. It seems to be getting warm in here," I teased her.

"Now that's a good idea," she said.

# The Long Walk

So, with that we both grabbed our drinks and headed out the door. The cool breeze was a welcomed relief. We took a break from buster mode to just talk.

In a welcomed twist to the conversation, Karen said, "I saw you leaving the complex last night. Nice bike!"

"Thanks," I said. "It's one of my few indulgences. I really love that thing." Feeling a little silly for talking about a machine that way, I quickly added, "Do you ride at all?"

Karen let out a good laugh. "Are you kidding! They'd *kill* me if I so much as *sat* on a motorcycle. You should see the outfit that they make me wear just to play baseball! Some kind of ice hockey padded metal wire goalie mask thing, all to protect my face. Talk about uncomfortable. It really detracts from my game."

I just smiled. "Ahh, the hidden price of fame, huh?"

Karen smiled.

Speaking of show business … "You know, I didn't even think about it before I suggested a walk, but when the time comes, let me know when you have to head back. I mean you must have some kind of pre-show routine you need time to do, right? Oh, did you even get to have lunch before we left?" I said in a semi-panic.

Karen replied, "Oh, I had something before. Don't worry, I'm fine. We have plenty of time. Our group is all settled in now backstage, so no worries. And while we're on the road, I always have one eye on the clock. It becomes second nature."

"Oh, good. A lot of performers are not used to outdoor theaters like this one. Out in the weather you can get dehydrated *really* fast up there under the lights. I mean, I'm sure you know all this. Just sayin' that I don't want to be the reason for screwing up your routine, and then having something happen to you up on stage. I'd never forgive myself.

"Some of the guys tell me that they can lose six pounds or more during a one-hour show just from sweating. You should see them. They look like they fell into the deep end of a pool by the time they're done. Then they chug down five drinks in as many minutes as soon as they get behind the curtain," I said.

Looking back, it should have concerned me that the only thing Karen seemed to register from this whole exchange was the weight thing. But I'm afraid that I didn't notice.

"Six pounds? Really? I wish!" she said with a soft laugh.

"Oh, I don't think so. It's probably not a good idea to beat your body up like that. Now and then maybe, but ..." I said.

"No, I understand," she said. "I'm always on Richard's case to take care of himself. He's under so much stress, you know, not just with the shows, with everything. You can't have the star taken ill."

Karen was just walking along after this last comment and, thankfully, she seemed oblivious to me staring at her for a few seconds longer than normal while we walked along, as I tried to read her face.

I hesitated to say anything, because I didn't want to upset the apple cart 10 minutes after the whole grinning conversation. But sticking to my whole "just be yourself and don't worry about it" philosophy, I just had to ask.

"Karen, speaking as a fan myself, what you were just saying about Richard being the star of the show. You *do* understand that *you're* the real star of the show, don't you?" I said.

Talk about a wild roll of the dice.

We walked along several more feet before Karen responded, "Oh, no. You might think that because you don't know how much Rich does. Everything, really. None of this would have happened without him."

Karen wasn't upset at all. She was mostly just speaking as though she were clearing up a misunderstanding.

I started in with the parts of the story that we agreed on, so it would not sound like an attack, which it wasn't.

"Oh, I absolutely agree that you couldn't have achieved all this success without each other. But you are the one that people come to see and hear," I said.

Her reply came instantly. "No, that's not true. They come to hear the whole group."

Still doing ok here I guess … just don't push too hard. "Oh, of course …" I said. Let's try a new approach. "But let me run a hypothetical by you to explain my thinking and see if this makes sense."

"Say you were doing a live radio broadcast. National spotlight. Prime time. Twenty million listeners expected," I said.

"Ok," she replied.

"So the morning of the show, Richard takes ill. Nothing life threatening, but he's stuck in bed for a few days. With a few phone calls, could you find another top-notch piano player to cover the performance? Maybe someone you've worked with before in the studio, who you know and trust? And remember, it's radio, so no one would see the switch." I said.

"Well, yes ..." she replied.

"Ok, good." I said. "So now for Richard's backup vocals. Same situation, a few phone calls, someone you know and trust, the show goes on?"

"Well, yeah. But I sure wouldn't be happy about any of this," she said.

"Oh, no, of course not. He's your brother. You love him. But you see how the Carpenters would still be able to perform live, and twenty million listeners probably wouldn't know the difference?" I said.

Karen churned on this for a minute. I thought that she was still hung up on the her brother is missing part, which wasn't really the point. But, finally, she spoke, "Ok, I guess I see what you're saying. Probably a few more people might notice the change than you think, though."

"That's true. But for that matter, for the ones who might notice something, could they also be thinking that live performances never sound *exactly* like the records, not being in the studio and all? That could explain the difference too, don't you think?" I said.

Once again, after a moment's pause she said, "Yes, I suppose..."

"Ok great!" I said. "Now a variation of the same story. Live radio, twenty million listeners, Richard is fine and he's at the show."

I could tell that Karen liked this one more already. "Ok, got it. So what happens this time?" she asked.

"For this scenario, everyone is there, but this time *you* sprained your wrist that morning on a motorcycle ride with some knucklehead who works at the arena where you just performed."

Karen gave me a long smirk.

I just smiled.

"Well, however it happened, sprained wrist, you can't play the drums. What happens? Does the show get cancelled?" I asked.

"Oh, no way," she answered without hesitation. "I don't play the drums on a lot of our recordings ... we have studio guys."

"Exactly," I said. "A few phone calls, the show goes on, twenty million listeners are happy."

"Ok, last and final situation," I said. "Live radio, twenty million listeners, Richard is all set to go. But this time *you're* stuck in bed, say with strep throat, so you can't even phone it in. What happens?"

Karen took a long pause over this one. Finally, she offered, "Oh, well, I think we'd have to switch to using a recording for this one."

"*Exactly,*" I said, one last time.

We continued to walk along as Karen thought about all this for a while.

I can't tell you how proud I was of her at that moment. Imagine having a conversation about such a central point in your life but, just as I hoped, she didn't get defensive or start treating it as some kind of personal attack. We were just having a conversation, and she was just thinking about everything that we said.

I was really building up a level of trust with her that I've had with very few people.

After a long silence, Karen started to speak, "So, are you saying that Richard isn't really that critical to this whole thing, because he can be replaced?"

Good girl ... she's still thinking.

"No, not exactly. When I said before that you guys never would have achieved the success that you have without each other, I meant it," I said.

"So, then what *are* you saying?" Karen asked.

"Ok, imagine this …" I said.

Karen gave me a dirty look.

"No more long stories, pinky swear," I said. It was funny how pinky swear always made her smile. I guess not many people say it anymore.

"Every group needs a hit, the more the better. It's really hard to hit number 1 with a cover song[6]. You guys did it a few times because most folks didn't know those songs that well from previous recordings. That, and Richards great treatment and arrangement of them," I said.

"So, he *is* important?" Karen said.

"Yes, of course! Richard is a genius with this stuff," I said.

I could tell that Karen was happy that I said that.

"Go on," she said.

"So artists need hits. New songs. Richard helps write them, or he finds them. Without more than one good hit, you get added to the long list of one-hit wonders," I said.

---

[6] A cover version of a song is a new recording by a musician other than the original performer or composer of the song. "Close to You" and "Superstar" were both Carpenters major hits using existing songs.

"Yup," Karen piped in.

"Ok, now think about the success of Elton John[7] for a minute." I said.

"I love his work," Karen replied.

"Oh, I know, so do I. He's second only to you in my mind," I said. "Well, and maybe Joni Mitchell[8]."

Karen smiled at that.

"So who is in Elton John's band?" I asked.

"Oh, I don't know. I did see him once though. What a performer," she said.

"I agree," I added. "So another question then. Who helps write Elton's songs?"

"That's Bernie. Bernie Taupin," she said.

"Yes, it is. One of the best song writing teams there is. But how many people know Bernie?" I said.

"No, you're right," Karen replied. "I know of him because I'm in the business, but most folks wouldn't."

---

[7] Elton John is a British singer, pianist, and composer, with over 50 songs on the Billboard Top 40 list.

[8] Joni Mitchell is one of the most influential singer-songwriters to emerge from the 1960s. Over the years she has won 11 Grammy Awards and was inducted into the Rock and Roll Hall of Fame in 1997.

"Bernie brings a lot of the same skills to their song writing success that Richard and his team do to yours," I said. "But he's not Elton John's brother is he, so few people know him, and his name is not hanging up in lights next to Elton's. Folks are going to the shows to hear 'Elton John'."

I stopped talking just then, thinking that I had probably already said too much. I was really trying to let Karen think things through and reach her own conclusion about her critical role in the group, rather than giving her an opinion and have her dismiss it out of hand like before, without giving it any additional thought. But enough is enough.

We continued to walk along quietly for several minutes while Karen seemed to be thinking about everything we said. I wanted to change the topic, but my mind was drawing a blank as I struggled to quickly find something else to talk about. I had no way of knowing that a new topic was waiting for us just around the bend.

# Gossip Man

No sooner had we rounded the corner into the back parking area then a familiar smell hit me, except that this time it hit me more like a ton of bricks. Cigar smoke. It was Wayne.

"Oh, God," I mumbled under my breath, as I clutched my forehead with my hand and I tilted my head down, as if trying to hide my face.

"Is something wrong?" Karen asked.

"Yes, big time. That's my friend Wayne over in the gatehouse. He's the world's biggest gossip. I love the man, I really do, but his whole life revolves around juicy scandals. He really should be working at The National Enquirer, not here," I said.

It only took a moment for us to reach the gatehouse, where Wayne stood smiling. "Oh great," I thought, another grinner.

Just as we were about to reach the gatehouse door, Karen threw her arms around my neck and started hanging off me, half leaning up against me as we walked.

"Hi, Wayne!" she said.

I think the only reason that Wayne didn't see the startled look on my face is because Karen's greeting left him more stunned than I was.

"Misss Carpenter ..." he stammered. "Why, hello."

"Karen. Please," she said.

"Hello, *Karen*," he said, almost afraid to say the word.

"You know my boyfriend, John, don't you?" she said. And with that she planted a big kiss on my cheek.

What a devil! She enjoyed watching me squirm.

"So, you keeping us safe today?" she said.

"Yes, ma'am," he said. "I mean Karen." This time he managed to to say her name without hesitating.

Slowly recovering from the surprise visit, Wayne started to speak, "So what are you two kids up to on this beautiful day?"

Before I could even think of anything safe to say, Karen jumped in, "We're just out looking for a quiet place to kiss."

Wayne's eyes seemed to bug out of his head when he heard that one.

"Don't listen to her," I said. "I think she's drunk."

Oh, no! Talk about accidentally adding fuel to the fire. Wayne was getting excited over all this great gossip. Drunken musicians!

"I'm only kidding," I said. "She's just getting even with me for picking on her brother."

Karen let out a chuckle.

"We'd better get going," I said, first taking the opportunity to get rid of our empty drink cups in the gatehouse trash bin.

"See ya later," I said.

"Bye, Wayne!" Karen added with a grin.

Wayne just smiled and waved.

As we got out of earshot of the gatehouse, I turned to her and said, "What are you *doing* woman? Are you insane!?"

Karen was doubled over in laughter, her left hand covering her mouth, and her right arm was clutching her stomach. As she tried to muster the energy to speak but couldn't, she started pointing at me, but still laughing.

"You should have seen your face!" she howled.

"You *like* embarrassing people, don't you!" I said.

"Well, not everyone. You're more fun than most! Your face is still beet red, ya know!" she added.

"That's not from embarrassment," I quickly shot back. "That's from the surprise kiss!"

"Same difference, it sounds like to me!" Karen laughed.

Recovering my composure a bit, I quietly started to scold her. "You *do* realize, of course, that by this time tomorrow this whole story will be all around the campus, don't you?" I said.

I was having trouble keeping a straight face by this point, fighting the smile that wanted to come out. But she already knew that the stern tone in my voice was all for show.

"Oh, I don't care," she said. "It was funny. Anyway," she added, "I never get to control anything. It's about time I started to at least control the gossip about me, don't you think?"

I just shook my head in wonder!

After all this excitement, we walked along for a while, not saying anything, both just settling down from all the fun but still feeling good.

After a block or so, Karen turned to me and said, "So tell me something about *you.*"

"Oh, gee, where to start," I said after a few seconds, thinking about the question.

"Well, tell me about that song title trick you did the other day when I met you. After just a *single* note? That was pretty impressive, you know, in or out of the business," Karen said.

"Oh, it's no trick at all, it's just something that I can do. I've always had a great memory. Danny likes to use it to make bar bets with strangers," I said.

"But *how* do you do it?" she said.

"I don't really know, to be honest. I just do. I mean, if I asked you how do you sing in three octaves, how would you explain it?" I said.

Karen nodded, "I understand. So it's a gift then," she said.

"Yes, I suppose it is," I said. After a few seconds I quipped "It's just not as marketable as your gift."

Karen smiled and said, "I used to do something kinda similar with baseball statistics when I was younger."

"Really? Now that's something I would never have guessed in a million years. Which team?" I asked.

"Well, I like the Yankees, but I knew a lot of stats. No bets! It was just for fun. But I would get more things right than most boys, though," she said.

"Oh, I thought you might have been teasing before with that baseball mask story, how it was cramping your game style," I said.

"Heck, no," she said. "I know what I'm doing out on the field!"

"Well, FYI, baseball knowledge is sacred territory for guys. It's tied very closely to masculinity and ego, so tread lightly there, sister," I said in a very teasing manner.

"Yeah, you guys are a fragile bunch, ain't you!" she said.

I nodded in agreement.

"You should have seen the effort it took me to get on the drumline at school. 'Girls don't do that' they told me," she said.

"You showed 'em?" I asked.

"I showed them big time! Soon I was better than most all the guys," Karen said.

"Yes, I saw that you punctured a few egos with your high rating in the Playboy magazine best drummer[9] list back in February," I said.

"Playboy, huh?" she said suspiciously.

"Yes … er, well I just *had* to know how you did on the survey," I said.

"Right," she said with a grin.

"Well done, though," I added.

Karen smiled and said, "So do you *have* a favorite drummer?"

"*Besides* you?" I asked.

"*… of course*," she shot back.

"Probably Dino Danelli of The Rascals[10] … and not just because he's a Jersey boy! He's good. But very underrated in my opinion," I said.

Karen smiled and nodded.

"Oh, and hey," I added.

---

[9] Karen came in at number 10 of the top 25 entries in the 1975 survey. Some of the lower ranking guys bitched loudly about being ranked behind "a girl."

[10] "The Rascals" were a rock group formed in Garfield, New Jersey, in 1965. Between 1966 and 1968 they reached the top 20 of the Billboard Hot 100 songs with nine singles. The band was inducted into the Rock and Roll Hall of Fame in 1997.

Karen looked over at me.

"The Rascals seemed to do *just fine* with their lead singer sitting behind a keyboard," I said.

"*Thank You*[11]," Karen replied.

After a few moment's pause, Karen continued, "So you haven't found anything that you can use this special memory thing with?"

"Well, I start school for computers in September: Information Technology," I said. "So, hopefully it will be of benefit there. But I can always fall back on making music quiz bar bets with Danny or maybe enter contests like Ralph Kramden did to try and win prize money."

Karen enjoyed that last one and she understood the reference to that old "The Honeymooners[12]" episode.

"You really *do* like old shows and movies, don't you?" she said.

---

[11] Karen Carpenter always considered herself a drummer first, and a singer second. Initially Karen did all her singing from behind the drums, but some in the audience couldn't see her well on stage sitting there. As the group's fame rose, she was essentially forced to come out from behind the drums to sing center stage, and delegate most of the drumming work to someone else. Being out front terrified Karen, and many believe that this change may have been the beginning of her health struggles, leading to her premature death.

[12] "The Honeymooners" was an early TV sitcom from the mid-1950s. In one episode, Ralph Kramden, one of the main characters on the show, enters a name-that-tune contest but gets so nervous that he loses.

"I do. When I want to relax, it's the perfect escape. It's one of the few things that can turn my mind off for a little while," I said.

"I like them, too," she replied.

"So what about the music part? You know a lot more than most civilians," she said.

I smiled at that one. She can't help being a buster.

"I *do* love my music, yes," I said.

"Can you sing?" she asked.

I laughed. "I can't sing to save my life! But I wish more than anything that I could," I said.

"Show me," she said.

"Oh, no. Trust me. You *really* don't want me to do this," I replied.

"*Show me!*" she said again. "I'm a professional singer, I can help you."

With that I sang the first line of her "Superstar" song for her.

After a moment's pause she turned toward me and said, "Oh, dear ... I *can't* help you."

Slowly a most mischievous look came over her face. Karen had the most expressive face of anyone I think I've ever met, especially her eyes. And she used it well. She could share a hundred different feelings without saying a single word.

"I told you!" I said. "Believe me, if I found Aladdin's lamp[13] and got three wishes, my very first wish would be to have a beautiful singing voice."

As we walked along, I could tell that Karen was thinking about this whole wish thing, probably because it's not something that she ever had to consider before, being such a gifted singer herself.

Finally, she asked, "So whose voice would you pick?"

"Ah, now there's a question," I said. "Honestly, if this were all really happening, it would probably take me a week to decide. But since this one is just for 'practice,' I'd probably say Gary Puckett[14]. He'd be on my top ten list no matter what."

"Gary's good," she said. "But why him?"

"Gary has a pitch-perfect voice. I mean the clarity. Down to the word. Down to the syllable. You hear it all," I said.

Karen nodded knowingly.

"That's actually what I love about your voice, too," I added.

---

[13] A magical object that allows its owner to make wishes and have them granted.

[14] Lead vocalist for "Gary Puckett & The Union Gap," a musical group that had six consecutive gold records in 1968.

"Thank you," she said.

Her reply didn't sound mechanical at all this time.

"Voice aside, I'm not as big a fan of many of his song selections. I guess I'm just not into power ballads[15]," I said.

"You didn't like our 'Goodbye To Love' song?" she asked.

"Oh, I *loved* it. I've heard people refer to it as a power ballad because of the guitar solo, but I never considered it one. But if it is, then I guess I just like what I like," I said.

"We got a *lot* of grief over that one," Karen laughed.

"I remember. Boy, I haven't seen people get so worked up since Dylan went electric[16]," I said.

"Well, I don't know if it was *that* bad! But I'm sure that there were more than a few fan club membership cards ripped up over that song," she said.

"But you *have* to experiment with new sounds or vocals. Music is always evolving. I think that's why I liked the song

---

[15] An emotional rock song with a slow tempo, dramatic sung vocals, and many instruments. Power ballads usually start soft, then heaviness builds up with drums and heavy electric guitars.

[16] Bob Dylan was a major acoustic guitar folk music singer-songwriter of the 1960s. He was criticized by other folk music artists and fans for moving away from political songwriting and for performing with an electric band starting in 1965, even being booed at several of his performances. Over time, his electric period has come to be recognized by critics and fans alike as producing some of his best music.

'Eve' from your first album so much. It was different. I just loved the string section near the middle," I said.

"You really *are* a fan, aren't you?" Karen said.

"Absolutely, since day one," I replied. "I mean have you *seen* the lead singer," I whistled. "What a babe."

"Easy, there. Don't get yourself all worked up!" Karen said with a smile, having reused my Bob Dylan words.

"I can see now that I'm going to have to wait until you get tired to ever win a zinger contest with you," I replied.

"You seriously think you'll ever win? You hang on to that dream, boy," she said.

"*Ok, truce!*" I said.

"Truce," Karen said with a smile.

She held out her pinky finger and we shook on it. Pinky swear.

"So, now that we both know who is the 'best', finish your story about Gary Puckett. What did he sing that you liked so much to pick him?" she said, with a smile of satisfaction.

I just shook my head, giving up.

"The song that he does that I like is called 'Over You'. Do you know it? I just love it. Even the oboe playing in there is just haunting," I said. "*Actually,* I would really enjoy hearing Richard's arrangement of that song, for you to sing one day," I added.

Upon hearing this, Karen made a face and reached over and pinched my arm as hard as she could.

"You stinker!" she said. "And after all the grief you just gave him before. You had him on his death bed!"

"I'm sorry!" I said. "Sometimes I just don't know when to shut up. I get an idea in my head, and I follow it way too far down the road. I sure wasn't trying to turn you against Richard or anything. I hope you know that," I said.

"Oh, I know that, stupid. But you *do* look at things from a hundred different angles, don't you? I can't always keep up at first. It's a new way of thinking for me. But I'm starting to understand it better. I like it, though. But thanks for clarifying that point about Richard anyway. I appreciate you saying that," she said.

After all this, the conversation quieted down and we just strolled along the path for another few minutes, just enjoying the day.

But then a question came into my head. "I've gotta ask you something, because I'll never have a better opportunity to find out," I said. "If you had just *one* shot at an important drumming audition, what would you play? What's a difficult one to do well and that really shows off your skills?"

"Well, what do *you* think is a tough one to play, Mr. One Note, I really Love My Music? You tell me!" she teased.

"Now what have I done!" I thought to myself.

After thinking about it for a moment or two I replied, "Well, I can think of several drum solos that I enjoy, but a good drummer can probably make anything sound good and look easy I suppose. Boy, if I had to guess, I'd say the drum solo in 'Take Five'[17]?"

"Not too shabby," Karen said with a big smile. "I'm impressed! That would be *my* world-class drummer test if I had to pick one."

I just smiled at the compliment.

"But I'm telling you right now, if you had said 'Wipe Out'[18], we'd be through! I couldn't have been seen with you anymore," she said with a wink and a smile.

"I'm glad that I didn't know so much was riding on my answer!" I said.

Just then we came around a bend, and the stage area started to come into view in the distance.

Karen said, "Well, this was *so* much better than my usual downtime routine."

"Oh? What's that?" I asked.

-------------------------------

[17] Written by Paul Desmond, and first recorded in 1959 by the Dave Brubeck Quartet, "Take Five" went on to become the biggest selling jazz single of all time and still receives significant airplay today.

[18] "Wipe Out" was written and performed by an American surf music band called The Surfaris. Released in 1963, it featured an energetic (if not technically complex) drum solo, and it became one of the best remembered instrumental songs of the period.

"I usually just stay in my hotel room and do needlepoint," she said.

"Oh, well, I'm sure you'll have time to catch up with that tomorrow," I offered.

With that she turned toward me and gave me a jab in the ribs with her finger.

"What was that for!" I said.

She just looked at me and said, "You know, for someone whose brain supposedly never shuts off, you *really* are clueless sometimes! Do you know that?" After a short pause, she added, "It's adorable though."

It would be a few hours more before I really understood that she was right about the clueless part.

It had been a wonderful afternoon, and I never wanted it to end. But, of course, it had to. We found ourselves approaching the artists' dressing room entrance of the stadium, steered here no doubt by Karen as we finished our walk.

As we finally reached the corridor into the building, I slowed down almost instinctively, as though some invisible force field was keeping me out. Karen was two steps ahead of me before she noticed that I'd stopped, and she turned around to face me.

She spoke first, "I had a very special afternoon. I'd like to thank you again for taking time out of your day for me. I hope you're not exhausted. I know you have to head back to finish your workday."

"Me? You're the one with the big night ahead of you," I said, as I nodded to my left, over toward the stage area.

After a few seconds she said, "Oh, I'll be fine! Well, I guess I'd better go. Bye now."

As she said this, she reached out with her left hand, briefly held my upper arm, and gave it a squeeze and a slight brush with her thumb. With a lovely smile, she turned to head inside.

I couldn't resist the temptation to see her face one more time, and I said, "Hey…"

Karen turned and gave me a questioning look.

"If it's not a big secret, what *is* your pre-show prep routine?" I asked.

"Oh, well, I take a shower, change clothes, and they do my hair," she replied.

"Amazing," I thought. "A low-maintenance superstar." As I smiled at her, she smiled back.

"Gotta run. Later, *you,*" she said, as she raised her arm up to point at me as she turned to walk inside.

# Wednesday Evening

I had no energy or interest in talking to anyone else at that moment. It's hard to describe, but it was almost as though the sound of someone else saying my name was going to break the spell that I was under and return me to reality. Silly, I know, but that risk felt very real just then. So I headed over to the stage area and started getting it ready for the evening's show. It was easy to stay busy there and to also stay clear of others, if I wanted to.

I never did see my boss, Mike, in my travels that evening before the show, which is just as well. In thinking about it, I was sure that the whole "when you're done with this, report back here for your regular duties" thing was all part of the act. I'll talk to him later. He is always one of the last to leave anyway. If not later, then tomorrow.

Even now, a few early audience members were drifting in and walking around, examining the view of the stage from where they were gonna be sitting. It was actually much later than I realized by the time Karen and I had parted ways for the afternoon, and I was feeling guilty for burning up so much of her day. I hoped that she was at least able to catch a nap before the show.

Time flew by quickly that evening, and soon the audience was all there and the stage was ready for Neil Sedaka[19], who was the Carpenters opening act. He was good, a

---

[19] Neil Sedaka achieved a string of hit singles in the late 1950s and early 1960s. His popularity declined by the mid-1960s but was revived in the mid-1970s.

seasoned performer, working on a come-back of his own career.

I always felt a bit sorry for all the opening acts. They knew — and everyone else knew — that almost no one was there to see them. But they always put on their best performances, and the good ones did their jobs well. The audience was all primed and ready for the main act to appear. All part of paying your dues, I suppose.

But in only a few short weeks, Neil would be fired[20] as the Carpenters opening act, after Richard felt Neil crossed him over a breach of entertainment protocol. And the industry buzz over the affair would slightly tarnish the Carpenters' otherwise squeaky-clean reputation.

Karen was wonderful that night, as always. I was able to hear the whole show from the sidelines, looking up as often as possible from whatever I was doing to catch a view of her on stage. I made a conscious effort to stay in the shadows, however, because I didn't want to break her concentration. She was a ball of energy up there, and I thought I was starting to understand why.

What I was saying earlier about how riding a motorcycle can blow all the problems and worries out of your mind? I was starting to believe that good conversation, and more importantly laughter, did the same thing for Karen. The

---

[20] The falling out came as a result of Neil breaking touring protocol with some celebrity introductions, as well as reports that Richard Carpenter felt that Neil was getting better audience response than he and Karen. The following year Helen Reddy would take over as the Carpenters opening act.

recharging her batteries comment that she made earlier. It was all starting to make more sense …

You'd think that this realization would make me sad, seeing how the real reason seemed to have nothing to do with me personally, as much as I may have secretly wished that it did. But for some reason I didn't mind. I took comfort in the fact that I was helping in some way that no one else in her life could right at that moment. That was plenty good enough for me.

My silly jealousies about her boyfriend had pretty much evaporated, too, by this point. After our time together, I just wanted to enjoy as much as possible any more of it that might come along. After all, if you had told me a week ago that any of this would be happening, I never would have believed it.

And I was getting back so much more from this than I could ever hope to give her. For me these were priceless memories for a lifetime, while for her it was the best way she knew to survive her grueling schedule.

As Karen wound up her performance, I started on the last few things left to do backstage. It was getting quiet out front by the time I was all done. I thought that it might be a good time for me to swing by and see my boss, Mike, if he was still around.

When I got there, I could see that he was at his desk doing something, so I quietly got into his doorway with my arms on my hips and an angry look on my face as I waited for him to notice me.

After a few seconds he looked up. He started grinning.

"Do you know how much trouble you caused for me, mister?" I said.

"What trouble? I did you the biggest favor of your young life," he said with a chuckle.

"No, you and that shitfaced grin, I mean!" I said.

I could see that he was clearly confused.

"That smile on your face. Do you know how much trouble that got me into?" I added.

By this time, I was already starting to smile at him.

I honestly don't think that he was aware of the grin that he had on his face while he was talking to Karen. He started to feel his jaw with his hand, as though he were thinking, "Oh, that's why my face muscles hurt."

"So how was your day? I haven't seen anything of you around the campus today. Everything go ok?" Mike asked.

"It was perfect, actually. Thanks for letting me do that. I know it had nothing to do with my job responsibilities. I actually feel a little guilty, like I was playing hooky all day on company time," I said.

After thinking about it for a second, I added, "Maybe we should make the install tomorrow a freebie and call it even."

"Don't worry about it," Mike said. "Keeping our stars happy helps the Center, so all's well that ends well. Besides, I think I've erased at least 50 hours from your timecards since you started here. So … anything that you want to tell me about?" he added with a wink.

"You mean Wayne hasn't called you yet?" I replied.

"You let Wayne see you do something? Oh, that's not good," Mike said.

"Wayne saw nothing. There was nothing to see, actually. I was just teasing. Miss Carpenter is a lovely lady. I think that she just needed a few hours of distraction to get her mind off of her work, that's all. She probably picked me because I was the only person who didn't run and hide when they saw her coming," I said.

After finishing my big speech, I realized that I *had* forgotten about that kiss on the cheek that Wayne saw.

"Well, whatever the reason, I'm glad it went well," Mike said.

"But tell me one thing before I go," I said. "Did you take acting classes or something? That was quite a performance you put on for me in your office this morning!"

"No," he laughed. "But I'll tell you what my secret is if you really wanna know. I had to put a pebble in my shoe and step on it every time I thought I was gonna smile. I had a black and blue mark on the bottom of my foot by the time you left here."

"Well, that explains the grumpiness. Serves you right old man," I laughed.

"Ahhhh … . Get out of here. You have an early day tomorrow. I hope you haven't forgotten. Playtime with Miss Carpenter is over, you know," he said.

"Yeah, I know. Dammit," I said with a wink. "I'll see you in the morning." With that I turned and left.

Mike actually *had* done me a tremendous favor this morning, and I don't just mean letting me go in the first place. If I had had any idea that Karen was waiting for me in building "A" this morning, I probably would have been a nervous wreck by the time I got over there.

In thinking about it, the three times I'd been with her were always a surprise for me, and I think that helped. Now that she and I have spent more time together, it probably wouldn't bother me as much, but this morning still would have.

After a crazy day, I took a few minutes washing up in the locker room before grabbing my gear to leave. I was ready for a good night's sleep, that's for sure. It was getting late by the time I finally made my way over to the parking area where my bike was to head on home.

The parking lot looked deserted. The audience members parked out front were all long gone, of course. Most of the crew as well. All the artists, too, it seemed, judging by their parking area. It was not a great night for me to be here so late, since I had that install to do early the next morning. But this job has crazy hours at times — part of the territory.

As I spotted my motorcycle on the other side of the lot, I was surprised to see what looked like a person standing there right next to it. Even though it was dark out, the sky was still pretty clear, so the moonlight helped fill in some of the gaps between the parking lot lights. But even with all this help, I still couldn't make out who it was just yet.

I always parked near enough to the gatehouse that I knew Wayne or one of the other guards could watch out for my bike. Harleys, after all, are a prime target for theft. So whoever thought about stealing this bike would have to pass right by the gatehouse before they could clear the fence. But if the guards weren't suspicious, then what was this all about?

As I got a bit closer I heard a familiar voice. It was Karen.

"Hey. Get over here, *you*," she said in her best mock stern voice.

There she was, leaning up against the seat of my bike.

Without missing a beat, I shot back, "Are you *allowed* to sit on motorcycles, young lady?"

By now I was close enough to see her face clearly.

"Where have you *been*," she said. "I've been sitting here in the dark waiting for you for 20 minutes!"

"Well, you'll be happy to know that I was just in with my boss, Mike, defending your honor. That's what took me so long," I said.

"Did you beat him up good for me, *biker* boy?" she said with a giggle.

"Well, if a severe tongue lashing counts as violence, then yes, *yes I did*," I said.

Karen smiled.

By this time we were standing almost face to face there in the moonlight.

"So, what happened?" she asked.

"Oh, I should probably save that story for another day. It would take too long to tell you," I said. Quickly trying not to sound like an old poop, I added, "You know, unless I leave out all the graphic violence, blood and stuff … and then we had to wait for the ambulance, of course."

"*No,* heavens! Don't leave all that out! But yeah, I know, it *is* getting late," she said. "They're holding a car for me over in the next lot, so I only have a few minutes anyway."

"So is everything ok?" I asked.

"Oh, of course. I just wanted to see you again for a sec, that's all. And maybe give you the proper thank you that I couldn't before, when you dropped me off at the gate earlier," she said.

Just looking at me for a moment — and letting me wonder what she meant — Karen moved a bit closer, and slowly looked down. After a few seconds she pretended to fix one of the lower buttons on my shirt with her hands, as though it had come undone. I looked down to see what she was doing.

Then, just as slowly, she raised her head back up, but at a slight angle, just to one side, until she was looking me in the eyes again. Once our eyes met, she stuck her finger inside the gap between two of my shirt buttons, and gave my shirt an ever-so-slight pull toward her.

I didn't need any more encouragement than this. We shared the longest soft kiss I think I've ever known. Just the one, but it was perfect. We stood there for a moment, just looking at each other.

I was expecting that something like a car horn from her ride was going to end the moment, but it was another thing entirely. Out of the corner of my eye I could see the glow of a cigar there in the darkened gatehouse, facing our way. Wayne! Does that man *ever* go home?

Karen followed my eye toward the gatehouse.

"Yes, I already visited with Wayne before," she said. "We're best buds now!"

I smiled and said, "Speaking of Wayne, I'm really glad that you finally found that quiet place for us to kiss that you were telling him about this morning."

Karen winked and said, "It was better than drinking, wasn't it, Mr. Clueless?"

"Touché," I said.

"Well, I'd better get going," Karen said softly, after another minute had passed. "G'nite."

"Can I give you a ride over to your car?" I asked, giving a slight nod over toward my bike.

Karen scrunched up her face and said, "You *know* I can't do that!"

"Hey, you can do anything you want in a dream, can't you?" I said.

Karen smiled and said, "G'nite, *biker* boy."

I stood there and watched her walk off into the darkness. A few minutes later I heard the sounds of a door closing and a car starting. I watched as I finally saw a car drive out the main rear gate. Time for me to hit the road, too.

During the ride home I thought about that wonderful kiss, and all my stupid ideas earlier about how Karen only needed laughter to feel better. It helps just like a bike ride. How I was glad to be there to help. Mr. Noble — yup, that's me. Blah, blah, blah … Boy, I *am* clueless about a lot of things, I guess. Well, mostly about one thing. Mostly about women.

But damn! Why is it that all of a sudden it seems to be working for me?

# Thursday, August 7, 1975

The alarm had to work really hard to pull me out of my deep sleep, but it was the day of the audio installation. Oh, darn! It took a coldish shower to finally clear the fog from my brain. A quick coffee and a buttered roll and I was out the door and headed toward the garage.

By the time my bike was warmed up, the coffee and buttered roll were gone and my riding gear was on. Off to work. The ride in was super painless. Zero delays. That was a plus. I was usually so early that delays didn't matter, but today I was punching a clock. One accident can add 10 to 15 minutes or more to your commute.

The thing that the other 49-staters don't understand is that here in New Jersey, we don't measure distance in miles, we measure distance in time. Heading south, for example, a 10-mile trip could take 20 minutes. But heading north, that same 10-mile trip could take 45 minutes. Knowing the miles was (and remains to this day) of no value. So if someone asks, for example, "How *far* is it from here to Atlantic City," the correct New Jersey answer is 'two hours'.

Even though I was spot on time at work, I could see that the delivery truck was already here and there was a flurry of activity around the back of the truck. I had no reason to feel guilty, because I was on time, but for some reason I still did. I skipped the locker room, left my helmet and change of clothes on the seat, and walked over to the truck.

Danny was the first to greet me. "Oh, sure, now that we're all done, look who shows up!" he said.

I was confused.

"Did I not get a memo about a time change?" I asked.

"I'm just screwing with you," Danny said. "You didn't think that 'pass' you got from everyone yesterday was still *good*, did you?" he added.

I wasn't following his train of thought at all, but I was soon distracted by what I saw, so I forgot about what he had said.

"But there is a change of plans," Danny said. "Look."

He pointed into the truck. There was a large sealed wooden crate marked FRAGILE, with two forklift holes through the side, near the bottom.

"Do you believe it?" Mike said, as he joined the two of us just then.

I bent down to peek inside the crate and saw only a mangled mess.

"Geez," I said. "What a sin. That's some expensive gear."

"We're not even opening it up. We refused delivery. The truck is taking it back for an insurance claim," Mike said.

"So we have nothing?" I asked.

"There was one smaller crate that was ok. I already unloaded that one. But they won't be needing our help this morning with any install, if that's what you mean," Danny said.

We all stood there for a few minutes, trying to figure out a new game plan for the day. I didn't have as much to think about because this was my day off. Screw the ride in, I'm outta here.

It was just about this time that Mike said, "Since we won't need you here today, can I get you to do something else for me on your way home, John?"

"Sure thing, Mike. What's that?" I said.

He pointed over to the table next to the loading dock door.

"See those two large file folder boxes and the manila envelope on top?" Mike asked.

"Yes," I said.

"I need you to bring them over to the Holiday Inn. We don't have time to schedule a courier. When you get there, look for a fellow named Bear. He's the Carpenters' head roadie. Give him the two large boxes. But the manila envelope, give that directly to Richard Carpenter. They are Arts Center contracts. They were supposed to go to the Carpenters' manager, but he had to leave early. So this envelope goes only to Richard. Got it? No one else," Mike said.

"I understand," I said. "But I've only got my bike here today, boss, I can't really take this stuff. Maybe Danny should do it," I said.

Mike was already shaking his head no before I finished.

"Danny got himself dirty carrying that small crate out of the truck instead of waiting for a forklift. He needs a shower as soon as we're done here. He stinks," Mike said.

With that Danny said, "Hey!"

Mike looked over toward him and said, "Danny, let John borrow the keys to your ..."

Before Mike could finish his sentence, Danny threw the keys to his Cadillac over to me. They landed in my hand with a klink noise.

"You scratch my Cadu and I'll kick your ass!" Danny said, with a grin.

"Hey — I paid for half that car with bar bets!" I busted him right back.

"I'll leave my keys and riding gear for the bike in my locker in case you need to go anywhere while I'm gone," I said to Danny.

I took a few minutes to ride my bike to the back of the lot to its usual parking spot near the guardhouse. Not a peep from Wayne this morning. "He must be ill," I thought. I headed over to the locker room, dropped off my gear, and went back outside to the employee parking lot.

There was Danny's one-year-old Cadillac Eldorado, in burnt orange metallic with a white padded vinyl landau roof, and an all-white leather interior. It was beautiful. His own pride and joy. I got in and drove back over to the loading dock.

By the time I got there the delivery truck was gone. I just pulled up next to the open loading dock door, and Mike passed the two boxes down to me.

Just then I heard Danny yell, "Shop Steward! Management doing Union work here!"

Danny was funny. We had no union!

I loaded the boxes onto the front floor of the Caddy. The one nice feature (of many) of the full-size front-wheel-drive Eldorado was that the floor area was flat as a board, all the way across. No "hump" like a normal car. So by pushing the passenger seat back, there was plenty of room for the boxes. They were clean, so it was ok.

I got in the car and headed over to the Holiday Inn. It was only about 15 minutes away.

As I got to the hotel I cruised around to the back side of the parking lot, looking for any Carpenters tour vehicles. I could just see them now, over toward the corner of the lot. And there were a few people standing around them too, just as I had hoped.

As I pulled up to the trucks I lowered the driver's window and said, "Anyone here named Bear?"

"Yo!" I heard.

"Bear, I've got two boxes for you from the Arts Center. Where do you want them?" I said.

"Right here. I'll take them," he answered.

I turned off the car and got out and opened the passenger side door. Someone grabbed the first box, and Bear grabbed the other one. As this second box flew by I snatched the manilla envelope off the top. Bear did a double take.

"This envelope is for Richard Carpenter," I said.

"I'll give it to him," someone else offered.

"No, I have to deliver this one to him in person," I replied.

My comment was met with silence.

After an awkward few seconds, I added, "Actually, I think it's bribe money. I saw a lot of hundred dollar bills stuffed inside there," I said with a grin.

Everyone started laughing.

"Richard was in the restaurant just a few minutes ago. Try there first," someone said.

"Thanks guys!" I waved as I drove off.

Good crew — these guys were very protective of their own. They were screening me to see if I would fall apart at the least resistance and was just making up an excuse to meet the Carpenters or if I was legit.

I parked Danny's precious car in an empty back row spot to be sure it didn't suffer any door dings. Then I headed into the hotel with the envelope.

The restaurant was just off to one side of the main lobby. This wasn't a typical continental breakfast hotel cafe with muffins and bagels. They served a full sit-down breakfast. They also had a complete lunch and dinner menu, too, along with a full bar. That's probably why so many of our visiting artists stayed here.

Someone told me that on Friday and Saturday nights there was live music and a really good singles turnout — in the 50+ age bracket.

As I got to the door of the restaurant I heard a muffled argument, and as I looked around the room for the source, I saw one person get up and storm away from a table. They were headed straight toward me and the door. It was Karen. She looked furious.

She also looked straight through me as if I were invisible as she passed by close enough to almost brush elbows, but with no acknowledgment of my presence. I was crushed.

After a moment's hesitation I walked over to the table, where a few people were still seated. Everyone was silent.

"Excuse me, Mr. Carpenter," I said. "I have a delivery here for you from the Arts Center. Some contracts."

Richard seemed to be really stressed, but not about me. He didn't even look up. He just sort of raised one arm up with an open hand, waiting for the envelope.

I placed it in his hand, said, "Thank you, sir," and turned and left. It was only as I was turning to go that he looked up and kinda half-nodded at me.

I made my way out of the restaurant, through the lobby, and back out into the parking lot. I just stood there for a second in the sunlight, feeling like a dog with his tail tucked up between its back legs.

"You idiot," I thought. "You were feeling like the king of the world last night after that kiss, but look at you now."

The truth is that any woman can do this to any man who cares about her, with just the withering look of her eye. But there wasn't even a look involved, and I still felt like crap.

I eventually made my way over to Danny's car so that I could get the hell out of there and go home.

Just as I was getting ready to reach for the door handle, I heard Karen's voice. "I'm sorry you had to see that, John," she said.

I turned around and lifted my head up to look at her. I didn't even respond to what she said. All I said was, "How did you know where to find me?"

"Bear told me what your car looks like," she said.

"I'm sorry," I said. "I didn't mean to intrude on your breakfast. I had some contracts from the Arts Center to drop off for Mr. Carpenter. They told me it was urgent. I'll leave you alone now."

As I turned to open the car door, Karen realized what was going on. She grabbed hold of my arm and turned me back toward her.

"No, *no*! Look at me, John. This is not your fault. It has nothing to do with you. I was in a blind rage back there. I didn't even see you. I didn't even know that you were here until Bear told me. He was about 20 feet behind you when you went into the hotel, and saw the whole thing. He found me on the stoop outside and he told me what happened," she said.

I looked at her for a second as I processed everything that she said.

"I'm sorry if I made you feel bad. That was an accident," Karen added.

Without even thinking about whether I should or shouldn't, I said, "I felt like a complete fool."

With that Karen started crying. "I'm sorry! You must have thought I tossed you aside because I didn't need you anymore."

She was hugging me by now. I was holding her too. Soon I was comforting her.

"It was my mistake, Karen, I'm sorry. I wasn't thinking," I said.

It took a moment or two for both of us to pull ourselves back together.

"Are you ok? I mean ..." I gave my head a single nod toward the Holiday Inn as I said this.

"Yeah, I'll figure it out," she said, as she paused for a few seconds to think.

"I'm probably the last person who should be asking you for a favor right now, but do you think that we can get away from here for just a little while? I really need to clear my head," she said.

"We can do that, sure," I said.

"I'll just run in and grab a few things from my room first, ok?" Karen added.

"Of course. Let me drive you back to the lobby," I said.

I walked her around to the passenger side and helped her in. Then we drove around to the entrance of the hotel, and I parked right out front.

"I'll only be a few minutes," Karen said.

"Don't rush. I have to make a phone call anyway," I replied.

While Karen went up to her room, I walked over to a pay phone to call the Arts Center and left a message for Danny that I would need his car for a while longer. I was already back in the driver's seat by the time I saw Karen coming out.

Just before she got to the car someone stopped her, but I could only catch parts of the conversation. The only two things I thought I heard clearly was Karen saying, "Tell them I'm going shopping," and "I'll be there later."

Karen jumped into the car and I pulled away. Her stress level seemed to have gone back up while she was gone. We drove along silently for a few minutes while I let her deal with things.

108

As we drove I was trying to think of the best place to take her shopping, so I started heading in the general direction of the Monmouth Mall.

After a few minutes Karen said, "Do you have a cigarette?"

"Try the glove box," I suggested.

Danny was a big smoker. Most folks were back then. I was probably the only odd-ball out, having never smoked a single day of my life.

Karen did find an open pack in there and lit one up to take a long drag.

"I didn't know that you smoked," I said.

Karen turned back toward me and smiled, "I don't really. It's not good for my voice. But it helps calm my nerves when I'm super stressed," she said.

I smiled and nodded.

But just then I did notice that the hand holding the cigarette was literally trembling. The poor kid. I don't think she really took more than half a dozen puffs on the whole cigarette. But just holding it seemed to give her comfort.

"Did I hear you say back there that you needed to go shopping? What can I help you find?" I asked.

Karen smiled. "No, I just said that to get out of there. I don't really need anything. But thanks," she said. As she looked out the window she added, "Is there anywhere that we can go to just walk or hang out? I could use that."

"I know the perfect place," I said. I made a small course correction toward the shore.

By this time Karen was settled into the seat, with her back mostly up against the locked car door, almost facing me directly. Her left leg was folded and up on the seat. She eventually put out the cigarette, and I had to admit: she did look much less stressed. I was glad it helped her.

But all this while I had been thinking things through myself, and I needed to say something before any more time passed.

"Karen, I need to apologize to you. I should have realized back there that you were dealing with a lot of other things at that very moment. I'm also sorry that I blurted out my feelings like that. I wasn't trying to make you feel bad. I think that I was still on an emotional high from last night in the parking lot, and the shock of the whole moment there in the restaurant surprised me like a gunshot from a friend. But I shouldn't have jumped to conclusions," I said.

Karen was looking at me the whole time I was speaking, and she was just studying my face in a slow, curious manner and half squinting. Finally, she spoke. "I appreciate you saying that. But I can also understand why you might have felt that way for a moment," she said.

"I just feel bad because I could tell that I hurt your feelings back there," I said.

Karen just smiled, reached over, took my right arm in her hand, and gave it a squeeze. "I'm sorry that the whole thing happened," she said. "Let's forget about it."

As if to change the subject, Karen started looking around the car and said, "By the way, nice wheels, John!" with a smile.

"This? This is disco Danny's car," I said with a grin.

"Well, that makes more sense," she said. "It's the perfect chick wagon!"

We both laughed at that one.

"Danny was just telling me a few weeks ago that he had one girl in here who was so stoned, she freaked out when she saw the floor without the hump in it," I said.

"Oh, yeah," Karen said, looking down.

"He had to stop the car and let her out. She started screaming 'What kinda freak show you drivin' man'," I said.

"Danny sure can pick 'em!" Karen said.

"Hey, don't forget that he was eyeing you up, remember? You're his type, too," I said.

"I don't really think that having a pulse qualifies as a 'type'," she said with a wink.

"Oh, you're *good*." I replied.

"So what do you know about disco?" she asked me.

"It's catching on big time," I said.

"Love it?" she said.

"The first time I really noticed was a year or so back, a song called 'Turn the Beat Around.' It was different. I enjoyed it, I guess. But two or three more songs like that and it all started to blur together. No, it's not for me," I said. "That and the beat gives me heart palpitations!"

"What about you guys? Do you like it?" I added.

Karen just smiled and shook her head. "No, I don't see us going that way anytime soon," she said.

"Oh, good, stick with the love songs. They never go out of style," I said.

"Hey, it works for country music!" she said with a smile.

"Yup, plus you get to leave out all the lines about dogs and pickup trucks. Those words have *gotta* be hard to rhyme," I said.

We both chuckled.

It was just about this point that the smell of the Jersey shore hit us as we got to within a mile or so of the beach, even with the windows closed. It's a glorious smell that's hard to describe.

As we came around one final bend in the road, there was the Atlantic Ocean, off to our right. Eventually we made our way over a drawbridge and then drove along for a few more miles. There was water on both sides of the road now.

The first two large parking areas that we passed were almost full, with people spending the day at the beach. This was the lifeguard section, where people could swim.

I finally parked, nose first toward the water, in the last parking area. This was the section of beach that had no lifeguards, so we had most of the beach to ourselves.

I turned off the car and we sat there for a moment before getting out. Karen was smiling as she took it all in. By the look on her face, you would think that this was her first time out of the house in a month.

# Sandy Hook

"The beach was a really good idea," Karen said. "Thanks, I need this more than I realized."

"I was hoping so," I said. "We've gotta get those stress buggers out of your system."

"Stress buggers!?" she replied.

"Sorry to get all technical on you. But you know what I mean," I said with a grin.

"So, what is this place? I saw Sandy Hook?" she asked, as we both got out of the car.

"Yes, Sandy Hook State Park. My folks used to bring us here every summer as kids. Miles of beach. I just love the smell of the ocean," I said.

"This reminds me of some of the great beaches in southern California. I love them," Karen said.

"I'm hoping that Danny has some sunblock in his trunk. He's always at the beach, too, so he might. I think it's his favorite part of working evenings," I said.

I popped open the trunk, and there was a whole shopping bag full of beach supplies.

"Ah, jackpot," I said.

I handed the sunscreen lotion to Karen.

"You'll need some of this before we head out. The sand seems to reflect the sunlight back up. You can burn in no time," I said.

Karen nodded. "Good idea," she said.

I picked up a handful of beach towels and turned toward Karen, "Think I should bring these along?"

"No, I don't think so. Don't give yourself things to lug around. We'll be fine," she said.

Once we both finished getting some sunblock on, she grabbed her hat and we started walking up the beach.

"You sure love your hats, don't you?" I said.

As I said this, she smiled and held the brim of her hat with both hands as she turned her head from left to right, pretending to model it for me.

"Like it?" she asked.

"I do. It's very beachy," I said.

"Well, yes, but it's more than that. It's my disguise," she said.

"Hmm?" I replied.

"Think about it," she said. "You're walking down the street and see other people out enjoying the day. You catch a part of their face, but nothing registers. It's what you expect to see — people out doing their thing, right? But these floppy hats allow me to get out in public pretty much anywhere I want to go, and nobody *sees* me."

"Oh, you mean 'Karen Carpenter'," I said.

"Exactly! It's great. As long as I keep my head moving and walk along looking down just a little bit, I can stay pretty much invisible, even in a large crowd. I just love the freedom!" she said.

Karen was so proud of herself! I just smiled. But it *was* a good idea.

"So what happened back there at the hotel. Do you want to talk about it, I mean?" I said.

Karen walked along for a moment, just thinking. "You know that drum solo I do toward the end of the show?" she said.

"Yes, your ghost notes," I replied.

Karen nodded with a smile. "They said it was starting to run too long. They wanted me to cut it back. They'd rather I did another ballad out front instead with the extra time," she said.

"But you love your drums," I said.

"I love my drums is right!" Karen replied. "It's like all the good parts of this are being stripped away. I just flipped out," she said. "But what can I do ..."

It was my turn to reach over and give her arm a squeeze with my hand.

"I'm sorry," I said.

Karen looked at me and nodded.

But I could tell that she didn't want to talk about it anymore. We just walked along silently.

After a few minutes of walking along the shoreline, Karen turned toward me and said, "So, any girlfriends? What's going on in that department?"

"No, nothing right now. I was seeing someone for a while, but that's long over," I said.

"What happened?" she asked.

"I was just young and stupid, I guess. I'm pretty good at that, if you haven't figured it out yet," I said.

Karen just smiled.

"I didn't appreciate what I had until I lost it," I said. "But I was just thinking earlier that you remind me of her in a small way. You both have such sharp minds. I mean you have to, just to think of those zingers that you lob back at me constantly, with perfect timing."

Karen smiled. "As long as it's only a *small* way," she said. "I'd hate to be the rebound."

I smiled at that one.

"You may be the biggest buster I've ever met. Do you know that?" I said.

"Bad?" she asked.

"No, not bad at all," I said with a smile.

"So was she always busting your chops, too?" Karen asked.

"No, that just seems to be your hobby," I teased. "There was one quirky thing she did do, however. Say we'd be having a conversation about something. You think it's over and you've moved on. A *week* or two later she would pick up with her last train of thought from that conversation, almost mid-sentence.

"The first time that it happened it rattled me. But it also seemed to turn on a switch in my head that has been on ever since. I started memorizing conversations like a tape recorder, to be ready for the next time it happened," I said.

"Sounds like the one-note thing you do," Karen said.

"Yes, exactly — music, trivia, conversations. All filed away," I said.

"And now? Any prospects?" she asked.

"Right now my dating life could best be summed up as 'Convenience' and 'Lack of Options.' I don't have much hope of finding true love there," I said.

"That describes my life to a T," Karen said. "The last four years or so, anyway. I didn't realize that there was a name for it," she said.

"So is this Terry guy the one? How's that going?" I asked.

"I *think* so," she replied. "He has so many good qualities. But in a lot of ways, we're very different people. He likes late evening gourmet meals. I enjoy that, too. But I'm also happy eating dinner in front of the TV, which would be difficult, because he doesn't even own one!"

"Seriously? That would be considered child abuse where I grew up!" I said.

"Yup!" she replied. "So we'll see what happens. I'm on the road half of the year right now, so other than meeting up in some city along the way or phone calls, it's sorta going month to month."

"Yes I do see you as more of a pizza and Pepsi girl," I said.

Karen smiled, "Oh, don't get me wrong, I like a good life. But I still pick and choose what's important."

After a few more minutes of walking, she said, "Can I ask you something about Terry?"

I turned toward her to listen.

"The other day when I was talking about him, did that bother you?" she said.

I got a very embarrassed look on my face right at that moment.

"No, it's ok," Karen said. "We're just talking."

"I'm sorry. I was really hoping that I hid that one. I kinda forgot about it already. But I was actually caught off guard by my own reaction that day. Embarrassed by it really," I said.

"Remember the other day when I said that I could see the gears spinning in your head at one point? That was the time," Karen said. "You hid it very well, but there was one thing that gave you away. Your eyes," she said. "They were moving from side to side, but they would never stop on me."

"Well, you're very observant. Yes, I was probably too ashamed by my own reaction to look at you," I said. "I spent several hours tossing and turning that night over that very question, because I had absolutely no right to be jealous. But I was..."

"Did you come up with any answers?" she asked.

"I did, yes," I said. "At least to explain it to myself."

"What did you figure out?" she asked.

"Well, long story short, a lot of fans have an imaginary life built up around their dream celebrity. You imagine how happy you'd be if this person were in your life. How perfect it would all be if you were together. But, of course, it's all one big fantasy. And you *know* that it is. But you're happy to live with this lie because you think, 'Well it *could* happen just this way.' And then some inconvenient truth pops up and bursts that fantasy world. That's what happened to me that day when you mentioned your boyfriend. But my shock was that I didn't even realize that I had built up a fantasy world at all," I said.

"About me?" Karen asked.

I nodded my head yes as I continued to look down.

"I can see all this being true. It does make sense," Karen said. "It doesn't explain the crazy fans, but I think I have more sympathy now for some of the regular ones."

I smiled and said, "Thank you. Oh, and the explanation for the crazy fans is — they're crazy!"

Karen smiled and nodded.

"I can't even imagine the things that you've experienced since you guys took off," I said. "And not just the fans."

"No one is ever ready for it," Karen said. "I mean you think about it and imagine how it will be. But it's still way different."

"And you're on the road half the year? How many shows does that work out to?" I asked.

"Try almost 200," she said.

"That doesn't sound very glamorous at all," I said. "So what's the long-term plan? Gonna slow down to six weeks in Vegas and then a show here and there, like Frank Sinatra does? Or is there a number in the bank you're holding out for first?"

"No. Not yet. Not right now. I enjoy performing," she said.

"Any regrets? You know, 'If I knew then what I know now' kinda stuff?" I said.

"For the most part, no. But lately I've been thinking more and more about all the things I gave up to be here. That's the stuff you're *never* prepared for. The tradeoffs," she said. "The thousand big and little things that will never be the same in your life."

"I would think this kind of touring schedule would burn you out though," I said.

"It is. It's cutting into the recording side of our work, for one thing. There's just not enough time to do everything well," she said.

"Do you get involved in the songwriting part at all?" I asked.

"Very little. Certainly not like Rich and the guys. But sometimes the songs come through with placeholder verses, where they're still hoping to think of something better. Sometimes we do, and sometimes those placeholders stay. And we make tweaks, too, depending on how the song sounds in the studio when I sing it. Every now and then one of us says something off the top of our head, and it turns into the 'hook'[21] for a whole new song. So it varies," she said.

After a brief pause, I ventured to ask, "So tell me. What was that kiss about last night?"

"You didn't like it?" she said with a smile.

---

[21] A song hook is a short lyrical line or melodic phrase used to catch the listener's ear and make a song engaging. It's attention grabbing, catchy, and makes the song memorable.

"Oh, I liked it a lot, believe me," I said.

"I don't know, really. You've been a perfect gentleman with me, and I've been having *such* a great time. It just felt right. I wanted to very much," Karen said.

"You aren't pushy like some guys, where every third sentence is filled with innuendo. Guys like your friend Danny are shooting for the hoop so hard that they don't understand that they're doing it all wrong. At least with some women. You have to start with the mind. If you seduce the mind, the body comes willingly," she added.

"But don't tell Danny I told you that! It probably wouldn't help him anyway, if you're not able to have a real conversation with a girl," she said.

After a short pause, I said, "The hoop?"

Karen just smiled.

"Well, you're right, though," I said. "I wasn't raised that way. I really like you Karen, a lot I mean. In any other situation I probably would've acted on it much sooner myself, but there was still a little bit of the celebrity factor holding me back, even with your clueless hint yesterday."

Karen smiled.

"But people have been fired at work for mistaking a smile from a celebrity as encouragement to flirt. I've never met anyone who is as big a buster as you, but having fun and being interested are two way different things. I didn't want to read too much into it, just in case it was all in my head," I said.

"I wish you could forget about all that celebrity stuff. I thought maybe you had," she said.

"As of last night, yes. I'm pretending that we met in 1969, pre-fame, and that we're having a date. Just two regular people," I said.

"Yes, I wish that I had met you back then, too, now that I think about it. Things would all be so much simpler," Karen said.

I continued thinking about all of this for a few minutes while we were walking along and blurted out: "Oh and hey … One last thing."

Karen turned toward me to listen.

"We shouldn't be too hard on Danny. If it wasn't for him, I never would have met you. That covers up for a lot of sins in my book," I said.

Karen smiled and nodded yes in agreement.

After another few minutes of walking, Karen pointed, "What's that up ahead on the horizon, blocking the beach?" she asked.

"Oh, that's Fort Hancock. It was an active military base until just last year. I hear that they plan to make a National Park out of it, but I don't think it's open yet. Still too much stuff to remove first. This whole area was used for bombing practice during WW2, so you'll see signs warning you to stay out of the sand dunes — live ordnance!" I said.

"Well, the beach sure is beautiful. So wide, too," she said.

"New Jersey sand is like fine white sugar," I said. "If we didn't stay closer to the water to walk on firm sand, that soft stuff would tire you out pronto."

"Now that you mention it, I could use a bit of a sit down. Why don't we take a break?" she said.

With that we both sat on the ridge at the high point of the tide in the sand, facing the ocean.

"So, how long have you been riding?" Karen asked.

"Since I was 17. I had a bike for over a year before I ever got a driver's license," I replied.

"I didn't even think about it when we were talking about Danny's car before, but do you even *own* a car?" she said.

"Oh, of course," I said. "It stays parked most of the summer, unless we hit a rainy spell … or I have the odd hot date."

"Who's the buster now?" Karen teased.

"Yeah, but my day isn't complete unless I can make someone else laugh, or at least smile," I said.

"You've been doing all right there," she said.

"With you? Oh, that's different," I said. "I just enjoy seeing that smile of yours, that's all."

With that Karen gave me a smile and a bit of a slow motion fist bump against my upper arm.

When you got to know her, Karen was very physically demonstrative. I loved that about her. I was starting to understand that there was so much more to it than I even realized, however. She often tipped her hand to tell you in advance that something was a delicate subject, almost as if she were secretly asking you not to hurt her. I don't think that it was a conscious thing on any level. And those clues were often couched in jokes or teases, so they were easy to miss. But they were no jokes.

It seemed to me that as much as she wanted to talk about some things, she was more desperate not to be hurt. Even from my limited time with her, I sensed that she covered over the hurt when it did come and tried to quickly move past it. But if this was true, it didn't seem like a healthy way to deal with stress, bottling it all up inside.

And at the same time, other things she would say were almost like unfinished thoughts. Things she knew to be important, but that she did not yet fully understand herself. Karen was very complicated.

"Have I told you about my new apartment at all?" Karen asked.

"No, you haven't," I said.

"I was just telling someone, so stop me if this starts to sound familiar. But there's a new building going up in the area near where I live. I was able to get an apartment there back in June. I can't wait until it's all done. I'm 25 years old, and I've never lived a single day on my own. Do you believe it? I think it's time," she said.

"Nice views?" I asked.

"There should be. I'm on the 22nd floor. City views, but still nice. And it's only a few minutes from most places that I already go," she said.

"It does sound nice," I said. "You need a place that's you to come home to, especially for as long as you're on the road sometimes."

"Well, believe it or not, that's been the main thing holding me back until now — the fact that I'm so rarely there. It seemed like a waste to even bother having something. But it's time. It'll be a shocker when it comes time to tell the rents I'm leaving," she said.

"Rents?" I asked.

"That's my nickname for my parents. Kind of an abbreviation," she said.

"Oh, right," I smiled. "I get it. What's your taste in decorating like?"

"Probably more California casual. Maybe a little French mixed in. Modern," she said.

"Well, you should have fun decorating that place when it's done. It sounds like it might be more of a contemporary building. Those can be a challenge to make feel all warm and comfortable," I said.

"I am looking forward to that part, yes!" Karen said. "I may need a small extra room just to store all my stuffed animals," she teased.

After a few minutes more of enjoying the view, I said, "Maybe we should begin working our way back."

We both started to get up, but the soft sand didn't help. I managed to stand up with the help of one hand, but Karen's foot slipped and she plopped back down on her tush.

"Here, let me help," I said.

I held out both hands for her to grab hold of, and stuck one shoe in front of hers, so her foot didn't slip forward in the soft sand again. She made it up this time.

We were standing there, still holding both hands and looking at each other. Using her hands, I slowly pulled her in close enough for another kiss. It was even better than the one last night.

With that, we slowly turned and started to make our way back up the beach.

After a few minutes of walking Karen said, "You know what. You're a good kisser."

"I know," I said.

Karen smiled and did a double take at that one.

I quickly added, "Thanks. What I mean is, so are you. It *does* take two. It's getting to be a lost art. Everyone is always rushing things," I said.

Karen smiled and nodded.

We continued walking along the beach.

"When we get out of here, maybe we can get a bite to eat. I ran out before breakfast this morning," Karen said.

"Oh, I wish you had said something when we left! I would have stopped for you along the way. I didn't even think to ask. I thought that you were already done with your breakfast," I said.

"No, it's fine. I'm trying to lose a few pounds anyway," she said.

"Really??" I said.

"No lectures, please!" she said with a laugh. "Everyone gives me lectures!"

Sensing that this was one of those touchy subjects for Karen, I switched gears almost in mid-sentence. "No. *No*, it's not that," I said. "But you're forgetting the first rule of landscaping."

Karen just looked over at me.

"If you trim the trees, the house looks bigger," I said, looking around to her backside.

With that Karen half bit her lower lip and gave me a punch in the arm.

"Are you saying I have a fat ass!" she said.

"No silly!" I said. "But you're down to your hip bones already, so anything else you lose is just going to accentuate that. Other famous people have been in the same situation. There are other ways, you know."

"Like what?" she asked.

"Take Katherine Hepburn, for example — beautiful, but flat as a pancake. But her wardrobe was custom tailored to give her the appearance of a figure. You just need a variation of this," I said.

"Well, I have tried layers and stuff, but I'm still not pleased with how I look," she said.

"I think that a lot of off-the-rack clothes are just going to hang too limp on you, and not help at all. Time for professional help, or new professional help," I said.

"Yeah, maybe ..." she replied.

After a few seconds' pause she added, "I don't know if I'm comfortable talking to you about this stuff. No offense, I mean, but I don't talk about this with anyone really," she added, with almost a teasing note, as if wanting to move on to a new topic but without it being awkward.

"I understand," I said. "But if it helps, you can always just think of me as your gay friend."

"Hmmm ..." she said. "You're not, are you? Gay? That might explain a lot," she teased.

"No!" I said. "I like girls. But you're not the first to ask."

"What did you *do*?" she asked sternly.

"Oh, I was over visiting this girl in my neighborhood who was just about to get married," I said. "I've known her all my life. Her husband-to-be really didn't seem to want to get involved very much in decorating decisions. One day while I was there she happened to ask my opinion on some paint samples.

"Feeling encouraged by a real answer, she pulled out a dish and she said, 'This is the China pattern that I'm thinking about. Do you like it?' 'Oh is that Minton?' I asked.

"She looked at me, and then looked to the left and to the right, trying to find the box. But there was no box. Finally, she said, 'How did you know this is Minton?' 'I *like* Minton,' I said.

"Now feeling really emboldened, she said she needed some ideas for her bedroom dresser. We walked over to take a look.

"After a few seconds I said, 'I think that this cloth doily thing on top is too casual. You need something a little more formal with this dark cherry furniture, a longer lace, with a little bit of a starched look. There's a great store in Chester for that, lots of stuff from Ireland. Then perhaps across the top, a crystal flower vase, a crystal platter, and a crystal photo frame, I said as I moved my hand from left to right across the top of the dresser.

"This girl looked at me for a moment and said, '*How* are you not gay?' I just laughed and said, 'Hey! I'm just trying to help!'"

"Crystal, huh?" Karen said, as if she were looking at me over the top of her glasses.

"What can I say? I like nice crystal," I said.

"And lace too, apparently!" she said with a giggle.

"Well *mostly* in the bedroom," I said suggestively.

I think I actually saw Karen blush!

Finally, the buster has been busted.

As we continued to walk along the beach, Karen said, "Well, I can see how you'd have some wonderful memories of this place growing up."

Almost as an afterthought, she added, "Were you happy as a kid?"

"I think so," I said. "My folks were not rich at all, but growing up, we never knew it. We always had clean clothes, enough to eat, and our wish was always wrapped up under the tree at Christmas each year. If there was a shortage of anything, it was privacy. Five kids spread over two bedrooms. But we survived. Oh, and no air conditioning! That one I'm not sure how we survived. What about you?" I asked.

"Oh, very similar I guess. But a little easier with just the two kids, I suppose," Karen said.

"So you didn't get into trouble a lot?" she asked.

"No, not really. If I did it was more accidental than mean-spirited. But I always seemed to be testing the rules, to see if they made sense. That probably drove my folks crazy more than anything," I said.

Karen turned to me and said, "Rules?"

"On Saturday mornings, for example, my mother used to do laundry down in the basement starting around 7:30 AM. I used to keep her company. I was about 5 or 6 years old. The basement door would be open, letting in the soft early morning breezes. But I was not allowed to venture past the top basement step outside until 9 AM. The whole yard was out there, just out of reach.

"I sat on that sidewalk as far out as I could, as long as my one foot didn't leave the last concrete step. I was like a fellow playing darts, leaning over the line as far as he could to get closer to the target. But I never asked why. But the rule never made any sense. I played out there all day, after all. Why did wash day have different rules?" I wondered.

"It wasn't until I was a teenager that I thought to ask my mother about it one day, and she just laughed. 'I just didn't want you kids making noise outside so early in the morning and bothering the neighbors!' she told me."

"Duh!" I thought. "But I had spent *hours* chewing on that one. I'm sure that I did a thousand other things like that, and kept my mother on her toes. But how does that poem go? Thank goodness a mother's love has no bounds?" I said.

"Huh?" Karen asked. "Oh, right, yes," she said. "And your Dad?"

"He worked nights, and he slept all day," I said. "I barely saw him except for weekends, during school months anyway."

"So what was your favorite show growing up? I mean I don't think it was really 'Gilligan's Island,' was it?" she teased.

"Oh, no ... not really! But I was a kid. I vacuumed up everything on TV. Just like you, I'm sure," I said.

Karen smiled and nodded.

"But I really enjoyed 'The Little Rascals,' you know, the 'Our Gang[22]' comedies? Watching them get into so many zany adventures, with almost no parental supervision. Some might even say that this became the model for my adolescent life," I joked.

Karen smiled. "So *that's* where you picked up your talent," she said.

I just looked over at her.

"For singing ... from Alfalfa![23]" she said with a laugh.

"Oh, you *are* a little devil! Ouch ... that one nicked the bone. Note to self: share no more deep dark secrets," I said out loud, smiling.

---

[22] A series of comedy short films produced from 1922 to 1944, about a group of poor neighborhood children and their adventures. The "sound" era films from this group were repackaged and run on TV beginning in the late 1950s.

[23] Popular child actor in the "Our Gang" comedies, known for his off-key singing.

"Oh, don't take away all my fun!" Karen said. "You're like my own personal private Bobo[24] doll. No matter what I say or do, you always come bouncing back for more, still with that same smile on your face! I can't remember when I've had more fun with anyone," she added.

"I can't, either, to be honest. You're one of a kind, Karen," I said.

"Thanks, Bobo," she said with a smile.

"Bobo, huh?" I said. "You really *do* love your nicknames, don't you? This must be the fifth or sixth one you've called me," I said.

"I do, yes," Karen said. "I'm still trying to find one that fits you. Nothing sticks so far. But no way has it been five or six yet."

"Alright, let's count," I said. "There was: 1. Mr. One Note, 2. Mr. Clueless, 3. Biker Boy, 4. Bobo ..."

"Ok, just four, then. No biggie," she interjected.

"Well, I dunno. The way you say it, I count *you* as another one as well," I said.

"Huh?" she replied.

"As in 'Get over here *you*', 'Hey *you*,'" I said. "It definitely rings of the possessive. Sexy even. I'm counting it."

---

[24] A child-sized inflatable clown doll, weighted on the bottom to return to the upright position when punched. Popular in the 1950s and 1960s.

"No way!" she said.

"Judges, how do you rule?" I said in my best gameshow host voice. "Ding, Ding, Ding, Ding, judges say '*Yes*'!"

Karen was laughing so hard her face turned red.

"You're insane, do you know that! Have you always been insane, or do I just bring it out in you?" she said.

"I really think it's you," I said. "I feel very comfortable being myself around you. And singing abilities aside, you don't judge, you just listen. It's hard to describe, but it's a really nice feeling."

"I feel really comfortable talking to you too," Karen said, as she gave my hand a squeeze.

"Thanks, Kasey," I replied.

"Who's Kasey?" she asked.

"You are. It's your initials, get it? K.C. You're not the only one who likes nicknames. I've been testing it out in my head all week, but I think it's a keeper," I said.

"I love it!" she said.

While we continued to walk along the beach, Karen was hanging on to my hand full time now.

I was replaying our last conversation in my head, when I realized something: Karen had me chatting away like a monkey in a tree. Guys always tease that no woman has *ever* complained that all she did was talk about herself all night on a date, but that's exactly what I was doing with her. But this was no ploy, she was just naturally curious. That and I secretly wondered if she kept the focus on others so that it would never fall back on her.

But I decided right then that I needed to do a better job at getting her to open up more. She just made the conversation so easy and relaxed that I'd forget.

As we got closer to the parking area, Karen pointed up to the hill overlooking Sandy Hook, "What are those?" she asked.

"That's the Twin Lights[25]," I said. "The only connected double lighthouse still left in the United States, as I remember."

"But why are there two?" she asked.

"To make sure that mariners headed into New York harbor didn't confuse this light with any of the other lighthouses located around the area. With one double light as a reference, they always knew exactly where they were.

"That hill up there is the highest point of land on the Eastern Seaboard, from Maine to Mexico. The view from up there is amazing. All the rich and famous people live up the coast a ways in a town named Rumson, but for my money, I'd take a house up there overlooking New York Harbor and the Atlantic any day," I said.

---

[25] The first lighthouse in the United States to use the Fresnel lens light. In 1841, two of these revolutionary lenses were installed, and Twin Lights became the best coastal light in America, serving New York harbor from the New Jersey side.

"What's the town called?" Karen asked.

"The mainland over there is known as Atlantic Highlands, but up there on the hill, it's just Highlands, New Jersey," I said.

"What a pretty name," she said. "I'd love to see that view."

"Why don't we grab some lunch and then head up there afterward?" I suggested.

"Perfect," Karen replied.

We made our way back to Danny's car and I unlocked it. I opened the trunk and sat down on the edge.

"Let's see how much sand I get out of these shoes," I said, as I removed each one to empty them. Hmm … more than I expected.

"I should do that, too," Karen said.

"Danny is gonna give me hell for messing up his car with beach sand. But it can't be helped. I'll top off his gas tank later. That always makes him happy. There's probably just as much sand tucked away in our pants, too, just from sitting on the beach for a little while. We'll be seeing sand on the shower floor for days," I said.

"Yes you're right … it probably *is* a good thing that we didn't fool around on the beach like I was thinking about earlier," Karen said with a wink.

"Not without protection," I said, holding up a large beach blanket with one hand, that we had left behind in Danny's trunk earlier.

"I think that we have a new name for you, Mr. Double Entendre," Karen said with a smile.

"What double? There was only the one meaning …" I said.

"I'm not quite sure," Karen said, "but I think I may have met my match with you. In the buster department, I mean."

"I'm pretty sure!" I said with a grin. "But wait. Does that mean our truce is over?"

Karen just smiled.

"So what are you in the mood for, for lunch, anything special?" I asked.

"Nothing fancy. Whatever's easy," she said.

"Do you like tacos?" I asked.

"Yes, my favorite," Karen said.

"There's a little place next to the marina that makes excellent tacos. It's just picnic table fare, but you'll have a water view for lunch," I said, as I swept my arm slowly in an arc, to show off the view.

"Let's do it," she said.

So we got into the car and made our way the few miles back up the island to the bridge that connects Sandy Hook to the mainland. It was still the same old steel and concrete drawbridge that had been serving the area since the 1930s.

Despite its height, the bridge still had to open when the taller ships in the marina needed to get in or out of the harbor. We didn't get caught by any bridge openings this time however, so we were soon over to the mainland side.

As soon as I cleared the end of the bridge, I made a sharp right turn to get back down to the water level, and then we made our way along the road that hugs the coast for a few blocks until I saw the marina.

"We're here?" Karen asked.

"Yup. It's right over there," I said.

Fans of today's food trucks would have been right at home at this place. It was basically a shack just big enough to cook in. The dining was all alfresco, with only some over-sized Sabrett hot dog umbrellas above the tables to provide a little shade. The ever-present seagulls were constantly on the hunt for leftovers. A french fry tossed into the air rarely ever hit the ground.

There were dozens of these June-to-September places in New Jersey, all built on the tourist and fisherman trade. Many years later Hurricane Sandy devastated the coastal part of the state, and all too many of these remaining places that had once been grandfathered in, or just ignored for so long, somehow got lost to all the new high-water building codes. It was the end of a much simpler time.

There was only one other couple in front of us, so we were soon at the order window.

"What can we get you?" they asked.

"I think a chicken taco and an ice water," Karen said.

"The same, but with a Coke," I said.

After paying we grabbed our drinks and made our way over to a table. Other than that one couple, we pretty much had the place to ourselves. And they were gone shortly, taking their order back to their car.

"They'll bring our order out in a few minutes," I said.

Looking around, Karen said, "This is nice. I love the slow pace. I feel like I'm away on vacation."

"The boatyard is a lot busier on the weekends. The taco stand, too. It's rare for me to ever get out here during the week like this," I said.

Just then our food order came out on a tray.

"Oh, good, I'm famished," Karen said.

"Dig in," I said. I took a long sip of my drink. That time on the beach had really dehydrated me.

"Oh, this is good," Karen said. "So, do you ever do any boating or fishing here?"

"You know, for as much as I love the water, I never have, no. Perhaps if I'd been exposed to it more when I was younger," I paused just then.

"When I was about 12, I went with my father and the neighbor boy and his dad out on their boat for a day. Just the four of us. Hitting the road at 7 AM. Stopping for hot cocoa on the drive down. Launching the boat. Fishing all day. Swimming. Right here at Sandy Hook, actually.

"I loved it. But that was the one and only time we ever did it. Each year I hoped we would go again, but we never did. I even saved up my allowance to buy my own fishing pole. But it's still hanging in the garage to this day, unused.

"I guess I still had not learned to speak up for myself or something, and just ask for what I wanted. And you really have to in this world, you know. No one else can read your mind. For all I know, maybe my father thought I hated the whole experience that day. But in reality, it was one of the best days we ever had together as father and son. I dunno …" I finally said, suddenly overcome by emotion.

"Oh, that's so sad," Karen said, reaching for my hand.

I looked up to see that Karen's eyes almost looked as though she were about to cry.

"I'm not sure what made me think of that just now," I said. "Maybe being here, by the water? It certainly didn't register with me back then. Not that I can remember, anyway. It's funny the things that can leave a deep impression on you as a kid."

Karen nodded quietly, "They really do …" she said.

We finished our lunch, and then slowly made our way back to the car. Soon we were standing in front of the car door, but still holding hands.

"You seem to have a nice life, John. I envy you," Karen said.

"Well, I do try to appreciate every day," I said. "But I sure don't pretend to have any answers. You're probably tired of hearing this by now, but actually I think you can sum it all up by one line from 'The Little Rascals'."

Karen gave me a "what's that?" look.

"The whole gang was piled onto some homemade 15-foot-long firetruck going down a steep hill, when Stymie[26] said, 'I don't know where we're going, but we're on our way ...'" I said. "That's life, in a nutshell."

As I said this, the smile slowly disappeared from Karen's face, as she seemed to be suddenly lost in thought.

"I sure don't know where I'm going," she said to me.

It was probably our first truly unguarded moment together.

I turned to look at her, holding her two hands in mine as I faced her. "Karen, this is your time. You have the whole world in front of you. But if you mean that you're not happy, then something is *really* wrong," I said.

"I'm happy with a lot of it, but I feel like I have no control over *any* of it. Not really, I mean. Like this morning with cutting back on the stupid drum solo. Nothing!" she said, with just a tinge of anger showing through.

---

[26] Another child actor in the "Our Gang" comedies.

"Everything revolves around helping Rich succeed. The whole family. But who's helping me? I feel like I don't exist when I'm home. If you only knew what I have to do to get a speck of attention from my m ..." Karen caught herself mid-sentence.

After a short pause, she added, "Sometimes I just feel *worthless*."

Karen stopped talking just then, realizing that she had shared much more than she intended.

I pulled her in close for a hug. She hugged me back.

"Does anyone else know this? Have you ever told anyone in your family how you feel?" I asked, as I held her.

Karen just shook her head against my chest and she said, "No ... I can't."

Looking at her again for a moment, I said, "Karen, you deserve to be happy. But it sounds like you've been putting your own needs second for way too long. You are such a wonderful person. And you give joy to so many people. I just wish that you could feel a little bit of that happiness yourself. It's all around you."

"I do feel it," she said. "I do. That's why I enjoy performing so much. For a short time up there on stage, I do feel loved. But as soon as the lights go out, I feel a little empty inside again. It's like I've become a junkie who needs attention like a fix. But if you only knew what I have to do between performances to get to that next fix, the endless compromises. It's just *too* much."

"You *are* loved on stage, Karen," I said. "But that's not supposed to be a substitute for the love in your own life. Oh, and there's one more thing. And this should be so obvious that I almost forgot to say it myself just now. Karen, you are a treasure. You're not worthless, you're an absolute treasure."

Karen started quietly crying against my chest.

I just stayed there for a few minutes, holding her by the side of the car as she slowly recovered. Thank goodness we had the whole space to ourselves. But I thought we should probably leave. Suddenly it didn't feel very private to me anymore.

"Come on, let's get in the car," I said.

She nodded. I walked her over to the passenger side and helped her in, then I went over to the driver's side and got in myself. Karen slid over and took my hand once again.

"I'm sorry. I don't mean to be a buzzkill," she said. "I'm ruining a perfect day. But I think the fact that I *am* having a perfect day just reminded me of everything I'm missing, everything I gave up. I think that I gave up my only chance to ever be happy with someone like you. I'm sure I sound like such an ungrateful brat. 'Poor little *rich* girl, she isn't *happy*'."

I looked at her and brushed the hair that was sticking to her wet cheek away from her eye. "No one would ever think that. You deserve to be happy. And you deserve to be cherished. You're a very special person," I said.

Karen looked at me for a moment, and then pulled me in for a kiss. But this time it was not a long slow kiss like before. She seemed almost in a panic, and I could feel the heat of her face from when she had been crying.

After a moment she stopped, but she continued to hold the back of my neck as she looked down and kept thinking. I was still holding her other hand, struggling to come up with anything else to say that might help.

After a few minutes, Karen regained her composure.

"I'm sorry, I don't know what came over me just now. I didn't mean to embarrass you by saying all those things I just said. I think your fishing story made me so sad that something inside of me snapped," she said.

"I think that's exactly what *did* happen," I said.

She looked up at me, hoping that I might really have some answers for her.

"It's the same thing that happened to you two years ago, when I made that silly voice, and the problems and stress of your day all came pouring out. I think the same thing happened today. But this is a lifetimes worth of problems.

"But between all the stress this morning about drumming and the small amount of extra empathy you just felt for me, it was too much for you to bear. You *did* snap," I said.

I could see Karen's eyes shifting slightly back and forth as she thought about all this.

"I think you're right," she said. "I do have a lot of stress and resentment built up in me. I didn't even realize it until I couldn't stand it for one minute longer. But I do feel a little better now. Thank you."

"I'm glad. But just remember that we haven't fixed any of the things that are causing this resentment inside you. You'll still have to figure all those things out. All we did today was vent off some of the pressure," I said.

"No, you're right ... you're *right*. I have to deal with things differently. Everything. I don't know how yet, but I do understand that I need to try. Thanks for helping me think this through," she said.

"Well I'm glad that you're feeling a little better at least," I replied.

Karen nodded.

I started the car and backed out of the parking spot.

"Are you ok? I mean should I just take you back to your hotel or ...?" I asked.

"No," she said as she shook her head. "I want to see that view with you first."

With that she gave me a bit of a smile.

"And I want to show it to you. Let's go," I said.

We made our way down along the waterfront, back toward the bridge area. I then took a new turn that would wind its way up a series of tight residential streets that clung to the side of the hill.

The route to the lighthouse was barely marked. There was just a small additional plaque on the normal corner street name poles, with an arrow pointing the way. If you didn't already know that this was the only way up to the lighthouse, you'd swear that the entrance must be on the other side of the hill.

After several minutes of driving we came upon the large gravel parking lot located exactly behind the Twin Lights. Before we got out of the car, Karen checked her face in the visor mirror and wiped one side with her forearm.

"It's ok … You look perfect," I said.

Karen was such a natural beauty. I don't think she was wearing a stitch of makeup that morning, so her tears had nothing to smudge.

Karen smiled and grabbed her hat. "Let's go see the view," she said.

We made our way into the small museum gift shop at the base of the lighthouse, and we got two tickets to visit the top. We started climbing the winding metal staircase around the inside wall of the north tower, looking out the various small windows situated along the route as we went up.

Eventually we got to the top level, went out a small steel door, and stood outside on the platform around the base of the light itself, almost 250 feet above the ocean.

Karen looked out over the wide Atlantic in front of her and just said, "Wow!"

The sun was sparkling like a thousand points of light on the rippling water, and it was almost hard to focus on it if you tried. It was at this point that I motioned to one side with my hand, for her to look that way. There to our left was the entire New York harbor, and in the background, the faint image of the New York City skyline itself.

For a moment, Karen didn't say a word, but her mouth hung open slightly as though a silent wow was still coming out.

"Wow," she said once again. "This is beautiful!"

I was so happy just to see the look on her face. It was pure joy.

"This is a secret place that we here in New Jersey don't tell most outsiders about. It's just for us. But I knew that you'd like it," I said.

Karen smiled, then she continued slowly walking around the whole tower, taking in the view from every possible angle.

As we made our way back around again to where we started, I pointed out some of the landmarks that we had visited today.

"There's the bridge to Sandy Hook that we just crossed to get back over here. Down there is the marina where we had lunch. Far off at the end of the island is where we parked and walked." And as I pointed out into the Atlantic I said, "And straight out there, 3,600 miles away, is France."

"Check this out." I said, as I put a coin in the sightseeing viewer.

Karen stepped up to look through the lens.

"Can you see New York City way over toward the left-hand side now?" I asked.

"Yes, I do," she said.

"Do you see that tower on top of the World Trade Center[27]?" I asked.

"Yes," she said.

"My good friend Artie Jones delivered that tower in three large sections, over the course of three days. Each day he drove his truck into the city from New Jersey with another piece. And each day that new piece was raised into place on top of the building and assembled. Artie is the fellow who taught me how to ride motorcycles," I said.

Karen took in the view all around, until the viewer ran out of time and she stepped off. As she did, she looked down for a moment and said, "Do you know what those large rust covered concrete blocks are down there around the base of the lighthouse?" as she pointed toward them.

---

[27] The Twin Towers of New York City. Destroyed in 2001 by a terrorist attack.

"Yes," I said. "That's the base of the old Marconi[28] telegraph tower. It was from this point that the first wireless telegraph signals were sent out across the Atlantic Ocean, back around the turn of the century. A few decades later, the tower was moved to another location."

Karen was just glowing as she looked out over the view. "I can see now why they call it Sandy Hook. That's the perfect description for it. And it's *huge!*"

Karen held on to the railing with both hands and just breathed in the smells of the seashore. It hardly seemed possible that just a half hour before she was so upset.

We took our time exploring the whole lighthouse, including the old lens turret just above the platform that we were standing on. We went back down the tower stairs and through the museum located in the lower section connecting the two lighthouses as we made our way to the southern lighthouse. We worked our way to the top of that one as well. Karen looked so happy.

I felt that if I had done only one thing right with her over the last few days, bringing her here was it.

Eventually we made our way down from the second tower and back outside, around toward the ocean side of the lighthouse.

As she looked back up to see where we had just been, she said, "It looks just like a castle."

---

28 Guglielmo Marconi, inventor and electrical engineer, known for his creation of a practical radio wave–based wireless telegraph system.

"Yes. It's the only lighthouse in the United States designed to look like a fortress," I said. "Shortly after this one was built, they standardized on a single simpler design, the tall slender lighthouse style that most people are familiar with today."

"How do you know these things?" she asked.

"I read it once somewhere. It's all parked in here, next to your 'Gilligan's Island' episodes," I said, as I tapped the side of my head with my finger.

"You're a nut," Karen said grinning.

We continued walking our way along the ocean side of the lighthouse, back toward the north tower. It was just then that something happened that I was quite unprepared for.

After all these days together with Karen, I had actually forgotten that I was hanging out with a world famous singing star. It was the closest thing to a normal relationship that I'd experienced with her.

But as we walked along, Karen turned her head back toward me just as a gust of wind off the ocean caught her floppy hat. It revealed her full face just as another woman was only a few feet away, walking toward us. In that instant the woman saw Karen, and she recognized her immediately.

The woman's eyes grew wide, and her finger came up, pointing at Karen, and she started to say, "You're Karen Carp ..."

It was at this point that Karen smiled, took the woman's hand and held it in her own two hands, and she slowly bent the pointed finger back around with her thumb, all while softly saying, "Shhh ... I'm on vacation."

With that Karen flashed the woman a huge smile and gave her a hug. The woman was *so* thrilled. She was actually thrilled speechless!

I realized then that I'd never experienced Karen's fame up close like that before. She was such a natural. And people truly loved her.

After this surprise, we continued on our way around the lighthouse, but I think she made more of a conscious effort to let the floppy hat hide her face by looking down more, having forgotten about her own rules while being caught up in the moment.

We eventually made our way back around to the parking area and to our car, and I helped Karen get in. I then got in myself.

I let out a deep breath, because I wasn't ready to say the words that I had to say: "Time to take you home, my dear."

Karen smiled and nodded, "I know," she said.

"To the Arts Center or the Holiday Inn?" I asked.

"The Arts Center," Karen replied. "Everything that I need for tonight is there."

We made our way out of the Atlantic Highlands area and back toward the Garden State Parkway.

We made the 40-odd-minute journey with hardly a word being spoken. Karen seemed to be lost in thought for the whole ride back, so I let her be. And in the silence I was soon lost in my own thoughts as well. Very soon I was pulling into the employee parking lot there at the Arts Center, and I headed over toward the stage area to drop Karen off. I parked in an open parking spot about one row back from the entrance.

As we sat there in the now-quiet car, Karen reached for my hand and said, "I want to thank you again for an absolutely perfect day."

That was all she said, but the look on her face told me everything.

"It was perfect, wasn't it," I said as I smiled.

She looked so happy. With that she put her other hand around my neck and pulled me in for a kiss.

"Try to get some rest before the show, ok?" I said.

Karen smiled and nodded. "Are you going to stay for the show or head home?" she asked.

"I'm staying," I said.

Karen smiled.

"I may run out and drive Danny's car through the car wash first. It seems to have gotten all sandy somehow? But I'll be back," I said.

Karen said, "Would you do me a favor then, and meet me back here after the show?"

"Here by this gate?" I asked.

Karen nodded yes.

"Of course," I said.

Karen smiled. "Later, *you ...*" she said, as she leaned in to give me one more quick kiss before she left.

I watched her walk down the path and enter the building.

Karen was like a different person. She was just overflowing with energy. Even her speech was different. Not that she ever seemed rigid or guarded before, but she now seemed to speak without any type of self-censorship. She looked completely at ease and trusting of the world, or at least of me. It was just amazing to see the transformation.

Before I did anything else here on campus, I drove back off-site and topped off Danny's car with gas. Then I drove over to the nearby full service carwash for a cleaning, including the interior and trunk. No reason Danny needed to inherit a mess.

After the car wash I made my way back to the Arts Center, and I parked Danny's car in his usual area. Time to give him back his keys. But I didn't get the ribbing from him that I thought sure was coming.

"Thanks for the loan, Danny. You're all fueled up. I appreciate it," I said.

"Any time, bro," is all he said.

"Danny must be tired from coming in so early," I thought. "This isn't like him." I thought that I might go find a cot in the locker room and catch a nap, too, before the show. As I walked over that way, my boss, Mike, came out of the building just as I got there to go in.

"Hi, John," he said with a smile, as he waved and passed me by.

Wow, another surprise. I found a fresh cot and I was sound asleep. Almost two hours would pass before the sound of music would wake me from my power nap. Neil Sedaka was just starting his set.

I was hoping that Karen got some rest, too. I know that I really needed it. I went over to the sink to freshen up as best I could, and then I made my way over to the stage area.

I was able to watch the entire show; the rest of Neil's anyway, but all of Karen's. I still tried to stay out of her view, but I could see her every action on stage. She was so beautiful. And talented. Before long the last song was over, and as the audience was headed out to their cars for the drive home, I walked over in the other direction to get my riding gear and to pick up my bike.

I was in no real rush, because I thought it would be at least another half hour or more before Karen might be outside. She still had fans to meet and autographs to sign.

I walked over to my bike and threw a leg over the seat. As I settled in I buckled my helmet. Then I heard a familiar voice.

"Good evening, John." It was my buddy Wayne.

"Hi, Wayne," I said.

He was walking the fence, but he just smiled and waved as he continued on by. Now *this* is getting weird. I turned on the fuel tap, pulled out the choke, turned on the key, and gave the bike a few good kicks before it roared to life. I let it warm up at a slow loping idle. There is nothing in the world quite like the potato-potato sound of a Harley exhaust.

Once it warmed up, I straightened up the bike and retracted the side stand, turned off the choke, turned on the headlight, and rode the short distance over to the gate area where I had left Karen earlier.

I pulled in to almost the exact same parking spot as before, about one row back from the entrance. I turned off the bike and fuel tap, took off my helmet, and waited for Karen to come out.

It was about 20 minutes or more before I heard a group of people coming out of the gate. There was a lot of talking going on, but I couldn't make out if she was part of the group or not.

But then I thought I heard her voice say, "Wait for me, ok?" And that's when I saw Karen peel away from them and head up the path toward me.

The rest of the group stayed exactly where they were, and they were dead quiet. I could sense that all eyes were on us.

Karen was smiling as she walked up to me. "Thank you for staying!" she said, as she leaned in to give me a kiss.

"Oh, of course," I said with a smile. "Another terrific show."

"I always look for you, but I can never find you!" she said. "But there *is* something I wanted to ask you, if it's ok?"

"Sure. What's that?" I replied.

"Well, if it's not asking too much after today, I thought that you and I might take another trip tomorrow. Would that be possible?" she asked.

"Yes, of course. My pleasure," I said with a smile. "What time should I pick you up?"

"How about 8 AM? Is that too early?" she asked.

"No, not at all," I said.

"But bring your car in the morning, of course, ok?" she said.

"Yes, I was going to do that. Where did you want to go?" I said.

Karen got a sweet smile on her face and then leaned in to whisper into my right ear "1969," she said. "Pack a bag, ok?"

As the full meaning of her words was sinking into my head, she reached over, gave me another kiss, and said, "See you in the morning, *you*."

She got about ten feet away and stopped to turn back around.

"Oh, I almost forgot. I figured out your nickname this afternoon!" she said. "I'll tell you tomorrow. G'nite!"

With that she did a half skip turn backward and walked off to rejoin her group. This whole time they had been watching silently from the distance. Karen rejoined her group, and they made their way to their own vehicles and left.

The changes in my life in the last 48 hours were almost too much to comprehend. But my head wasn't spinning like usual. For once in my life I had no idea what was going to happen, and I didn't really care. Tomorrow would come soon enough.

For the moment I had just one thing to take care of here on site. I rode my bike over toward Mike's office, hoping that he was still there. The light was still on. Thank God.

I didn't quite know what I was going say to him, but I didn't want to just not show up for work, either. That wouldn't be right. So I was just going to be straight with him. I got to his door and he looked up and smiled, almost as though he had been waiting for me. I suppose he heard my bike when I rode over. He motioned for me to sit.

"What's up, John?" he said.

"Mike, I'm in a real unusual situation here, and I was hoping that I could get your advice. Karen — Carpenter I mean — has asked me to spend the next couple of days with her, and I've said yes. I will be here during the shows, of course, to work — as will she — but otherwise we're gonna be out of touch. I don't like springing this on you with no notice like this, but so much has happened in the last few days that I don't even understand it all myself yet. If you'd rather I just quit here and now, I will, but that's not what I want. But I'll leave it up to you," I said.

Mike could tell that I was very serious.

"You care for her enough to give up your job, son?" he asked.

"I do. I'm crazy about her," I said.

"And she feels the same way?" he asked.

"Yes, I think she does," I replied.

Mike thought for a moment and said, "I'm really happy for you. For both of you. You do what you can around here while you're on site, but if not, don't think about it. We'll sort it all out next week."

I wasn't able to speak just then, but I think that the look on my face must have said it all. I got up to shake his hand, but it quickly turned into a hug.

"I won't forget this," I said.

Mike just smiled.

"I gotta go," I said.

Mike nodded. "See you soon, son."

# Friday - Saturday

It was still dark when I woke up early Friday morning. I hadn't had my normal seven to eight hours of sleep, but I was not one bit tired. I was too excited to sleep, thinking about the upcoming day. What did it feel like? My birthday? The last day of school? Christmas morning? Yes, that sounds about right! After a quick wake-up shower I started sorting through my clothes for the weekend.

Karen had said, "pack a bag," but I really needed to pack *two* bags. One would be my nicer street clothes for my time with Karen, and the other bag was for a change of clothes while I worked at the Arts Center. But even my work bag needed some street clothes inside, because I intended to shower a second time right after work and put on some better clothes for the ride back with Karen.

Toiletries were the only limiting factor. I needed enough for both bags. Luckily I had spares for everything in my vanity, so I was soon all packed. Shoes! Don't forget to take shoes!

I went outside and threw everything into the trunk of my car to get ready to leave. I don't think that I'd even started my car in the last three weeks, so I was happy that it started right up for me. I would have been in trouble if the battery had died while sitting.

I did a quick look around the inside of the car to make sure that it was clean enough for company, and it was. I normally kept my car very nice looking. I backed out of the driveway and headed for the Holiday Inn.

When I finally arrived at the Inn, I parked my car in the last row of the parking lot, more toward the back. Danny wasn't the only one sensitive to door dings. I decided to leave my bag in the car for now, so as not to look like a tourist when I walked in.

I made my way to the front of the hotel and around into the lobby. As I entered, I was starting to wish that I had one of Karen's magic hat disguises so I could disappear. I don't know why I felt that way, because I was doing nothing wrong.

I walked over to the hotel registration desk, and the woman behind the counter said, "May I help you, sir?"

"Yes, I'm here to meet Miss Karen Carpenter. Would you be kind enough to phone her room and tell her that I've arrived?" I said.

"Certainly, sir. And who shall I say is waiting?" she asked.

"Tell her it's Alfalfa," I said.

"Pardon?" she replied.

"She'll know who it is," I assured her, nodding my head.

The woman looked up the room and called the number.

"Yes, good morning, Miss Carpenter, this is the front desk. I have a Mr. Alfalfa here. He says that you're expecting him."

Just then I heard laughter coming through the woman's handset as she pulled it away from her ear because it was too loud! I could hear it myself from five feet away. It was Karen on the other end of the line, laughing.

The woman at the registration desk suddenly got a big grin on her face, too. After a moment she said, "Very well, I'll let him know," just before she hung up the phone.

Still smiling, she said, "Miss Carpenter asks that you wait here in the lobby. She'll be down to meet you momentarily. You can wait over there by the elevators if you like," she said, pointing the way with her flat hand, like flight attendants do when giving safety instructions on board aircraft.

"Thank you," I replied.

I walked over to the side of the lobby where the bank of elevators was located. Soon enough, I spied one elevator car that seemed to be coming straight down toward the first floor. I heard a ding sound just as it arrived at my level. When the elevator doors opened, there was Karen, still smiling.

As she stepped out of the elevator, she reached out to shake my hand, saying, "Thank you for coming on such short notice."

Not knowing if this was a new game or if she was just trying to keep things low key in the lobby, I played along and said, "A pleasure to meet you, Miss Carpenter. It was very kind of you to see me today."

"Of course," she said. "Always glad to help. Won't you follow me?" she added.

With that we both got into the elevator, and Karen pressed the button for the top floor. As soon as the elevator doors closed, she said, "Get over here, you knucklehead!" as she reached in to give me a kiss.

We were soon at the top floor and we exited the elevator.

"Over here," Karen said, as she pulled a key out of her pants pocket to unlock the door of one of the rooms.

As we walked inside she flicked on the light. "Holly cow," I said. "Nice digs."

"This isn't my room," she said with a smile. "Our manager normally stays in the suite because he's usually dealing with the press, photographers, and other business meetings. He really needs the space. Sometimes there are 20 people in here at a time. We did a photo shoot just over there early Tuesday morning," she said, as she pointed toward one corner of the room.

"He had to leave unexpectedly on Wednesday morning. We weren't sure if he'd be back or not, so we kept the room just in case. But I just found out yesterday that he's going to meet up with us in Maryland next week instead, so the room was sitting empty. I thought we'd be more comfortable up here and less likely to be disturbed. That, plus I've got the only key," she said with a wink.

"It's a great room," I said. "And an even better plan."

"That's why I came down to meet you in the lobby instead of asking you to come up. My room is one floor down. But it's much less private. The whole gang has a cluster of rooms, all near to each other," Karen said. "I already moved some of my things up here before you arrived," she added.

With that we did a short tour around the room to check things out. The suite featured a very spacious living room with a dining area off to one corner. There was a full kitchen, even if it was a little on the smallish side. There was a nice balcony outside with tables and chairs. Through the partially opened door, I could see the private bedroom with its own bath. There was also another half bath just off the kitchen area, near the entry door.

"Didn't you pack a bag?" Karen asked.

"Oh, I did, but I left it in my car. I didn't know what the plan was for this morning, so I thought I'd better wait and see," I said.

"Right now the *plan* is for us to head to that nice sofa over there and relax and get to know one another better. No Wayne, no Mike, no beach sand, no distractions," she said with a smile. She reached for my hand as she led the way.

—

It was just before noon when Karen and I found ourselves lying there next to one another, she with her head resting on my upper arm and shoulder. A smile slowly came over her face just then, and she turned her head slightly toward me and said, "So how did you know?"

In an instant I replayed the entire morning in my mind, but I still didn't know what she meant. So I just smiled and said, "What? Did I accidentally do something right this morning?"

"You did a *whole* lot of things right this morning," she said with a smile. "But that's not what I'm talking about."

"I think I'm gonna need a little help with this one. You kinda knocked the stuffing out of me," I teased her.

"Your nickname, silly! Remember I told you last night that I had found the perfect one for you? How did you know it was Alfalfa?" she said.

"Oh, no … say it ain't so!" I replied.

Karen just giggled.

"Why, you don't like it?" she asked.

"I wish that I had never brought up singing and Aladdin's lamp and Gary Puckett. None of it," I said, shaking my head from side to side, but with a trace of a smile already showing on my face.

"Relax, silly," Karen said. "I'm just teasing. That's not it. But it *is* 'Little Rascals' related."

Just then I closed my eyes, braced myself, and said, "Ok. Let me have it."

"It's Wheezer[29]," she said.

"I know Wheezer," I replied, as I opened my eyes. "I remind you of him?"

---

[29] Another child actor in the "Our Gang" comedies.

"No, he reminds me of *you*! He's always there with a cute smile on his face, not quite sure what he's doing, but happy just to be there all the same. You know — clueless, like you!" she said.

I just got a big smile on my face and said, "Karen, I think that my work here is done. Your reasoning is flawless. I can't disagree. Ok, Wheezer it is," I said.

Karen just smiled and said, "I'm glad that you like it! I thought it was *perfect*! But you *are* wrong about one thing."

With that I turned toward her.

"Your work here is far from done, mister. Come over here, *you,*" she said.

—

It was a little after 1 PM when I came out of the bathroom to find Karen looking at a pamphlet.

"Perfect timing," she said. "I was just getting ready to order room service."

"Oh yes, please," I said.

"What would you like?" she asked.

"Turkey on rye with mayo would be great, thanks," I said.

Karen dialed room service. "Yes, can I place an order for room service, please. Yes, one fruit cup, one small salad, vinaigrette, and one turkey on rye with mayo. Huh?"

Just then she glanced quickly over at me, and then turned back and said to room service, "Yes, probably. One iced tea, and ..."

With that she looked over to me and I held up two fingers.

"Make that two iced teas. Yes, the Lincoln suite. Thank you," she said, and hung up.

"What was the 'Yes probably'?" I said.

"They asked if you wanted bacon on your turkey sandwich, so I made an executive decision and said yes," she smiled.

"Oh, my twice-a-year treat. Thank you. What did I ever do to deserve you?" I teased her.

Karen just smiled.

"I'll be right back. I want to get out of this robe and into some clothes before room service arrives. Let me know if they get here before I'm done," she said.

"Will do," I replied.

While I was waiting, I walked over toward the balcony side of the room and checked out the view outside for a while. Eventually I turned back toward the room and continued my slow walk around.

Just then I noticed a pile of publicity photos on the corner desk. They were slightly scattered about, so I proceeded to neaten them into piles as I looked them over. There were probably several hundred, so it took a few minutes.

Just as I was finishing up, Karen came out of the bedroom. "What do you have there?" she asked.

"Oh, I was just straightening up this pile of photos here on the desk. Are any of these from your photo shoot the other day?" I asked.

"No, that was for an upcoming article. I forget the magazine. These photos are the ones that our manager gives out to the press. He was looking for one particular photo for someone. I guess he forgot the pile on the desk when he left the other day," she said.

"I love this black and white photo of you. It's perfect. This is more what you look like every day, when you're not being Karen Carpenter, the singing star. May I have this one?" I asked.

"Of course," she said with a smile, "but I can send you a better one later when I get back to California if you like."

"No, this one will be fine, thanks. I love it," I said.

Karen smiled.

Just then there was a knock on the door. "Room service," we heard. I let them in.

"Over on the dining room table would be fine, thank you," Karen said.

I gave the young fellow a tip as he left and closed the door behind him.

We sat down to have lunch. As we began to eat, Karen said, "You know you never did tell me what happened the other day with your boss, Mike. You know, the whole grinning incident. Did you ever find out what that was all about?"

I just smiled and nodded. "There's not much of a story to tell," I said. "I showed up at his door pretending to be angry, and he just started grinning at me, too! I don't think he was even aware that he was doing it with you. His face muscles were actually sore by the end of the night, so he got his punishment! He was just happy for me is all, as I suspected," I said.

Karen smiled and said, "Oh, that's so cute! What did he say when you told him about our plans for the weekend? You did tell him, right?"

"Oh, yes, of course. I wouldn't just not show up for work, even if he wasn't a good friend," I said. "I thought that he might fire me over it, so I offered to quit before he even said anything. But once he realized how important our time together was to me, all he said was that he was happy for both of us, and not to worry about it. 'We'll figure it out next week,' he said."

"Well I'm glad you didn't have to quit! But that was so nice of him though … I'll have to go visit him when I get to the site, to thank him myself," she said.

"I think he'd like that," I said. "And don't worry. Mike won't say anything to anyone."

Karen just smiled.

As we finished up lunch, Karen said, "I'm going in to get ready for tonight. It'll only take me a few minutes. You're driving me in, right? You did bring your car? Oh, no. You already told me that earlier, with the bag in your car," she said.

"Yes, I'm driving you to school today, no worries," I smiled.

"Be back in a sec!" she said.

As soon as she came back out of the bedroom, we took the elevator down to leave for the Arts Center.

Once outside, Karen and I worked our way toward the last row of the parking lot.

"My car is just over here," I said.

A few cracks and potholes had started to appear in the pavement as we reached the outer rows of parking lot, so Karen was looking down, trying not to trip over any of them.

She looked up just as I said, "Here I am."

We were about 20 feet from my car. Karen stopped so suddenly that her hand pulled out of mine.

"Holly shit, John! What the fuck is this!" she said.

Feeling suddenly embarrassed, she covered her mouth with her one hand. "Sorry. That just fell out!" she said.

There in the last row was my 1974 Lincoln Continental Mark IV, in white with a white vinyl top and white leather interior.

"Didn't I tell you about this when we first met?" I said innocently.

Karen just stared at me with a grin.

"Oh, I might have just mentioned that my Harley was my 'one and only extravagance and pride and joy.' But I guess I really have two 'one and onlys'," I said.

Karen just started smiling and shaking her head from side to side and said, "I'll say this much for you, you're full of surprises! Anything else back home that you 'forgot' to mention? An airplane, maybe?" she said with a laugh.

"*No*, I sold that when the hanger fees got too expensive. I wasn't really using it enough, anyway," I said.

Karen turned back to look at me.

"I'm kidding! I'm kidding! No, nothing else! Pinky swear!" I said.

Karen smiled.

I helped her get in the passenger side, and I got in on the driver's side. As we pulled away to head for the Arts Center, Karen said, "And I was busting Danny for *his* chick wagon! Man!"

"My taste in cars runs a little more conservative than Danny's," I said. "Orange isn't going to cut it with me."

"Yikes, this thing is a boat! It must be twice as long as my little Mercedes!" Karen said.

I just grinned. "It rides nice, though, doesn't it?" I said.

Karen started looking around, checking out the inside of the car, and she stopped when she got to the radio. "What is this 8-track Quadrasonic[30] thing?" she asked.

"Oh, that's a four-channel stereo tape deck. It really sounds good. There aren't that many recordings available in quad, though. You should get your label to do more of them. I can't play you a Carpenters tape, because you guys haven't released anything in this particular format yet," I said.

"I'll get right on it when I return to California," she teased. "Play one for me, though. I'd like to hear what it sounds like," she added.

"Boy, I think the only quad tape in the car is Iron Butterfly," I said. "They're not exactly first-date music."

"You really are all over the map with your music tastes, aren't you!" she said.

"I prefer to describe my taste as 'eclectic'," I replied.

--------

30 First generation four-channel surround-sound system. A&M, Karen's label, holds the distinction of being one of the few major labels to release quadraphonic albums in the early 1970s, but initially this was done using Sansui SQ (Stereo Quadraphonic) technology, one of several competing formats (think VHS verses Betamax). A&M then switched to CBS's QS (Quadraphonic Sound) format, before shifting once again to the JVC CD-4 (Compatible Discrete 4) format. In addition to these there was the RCA Quad-8 format. All these competing format problems were partially resolved in 1976 when the USQ (Universal Stereo Quadraphonic) format was developed, but by 1978 most labels began to discontinue quad releases of any type.

Karen just smiled.

"In there," I said to her, as I pointed to the glove compartment.

She opened the glovebox door, and ran through the eight or so tapes stacked inside, pointing her finger along the way as she went up and down the row.

"Here ya go," she said, as she handed me the tape and closed the glovebox.

The stereo started playing part way through the song that I had been listening to previously on the tape, but that soon ended and "In-A-Gadda-Da-Vida" started playing.

After a minute I looked back over toward Karen. She was still looking around out the window, but her hand was tapping the top of her thigh, and her head was nodding along slowly, all in time with the music. She looked over to catch me watching her, and she smiled.

"Yes, I agree. *Eclectic* is a much better word," she said.

The song was barely over as we got to the Arts Center. I pulled up to the artists' entrance to drop Karen off. Once I stopped, Karen looked down at the inside of the door, her hand suspended in midair, wanting to reach for the handle to open it. But she couldn't find it.

"Allow me," I said.

I scrambled out of my door and around to her side of the car. I grabbed hold of the door handle with both hands, like the military does for the President, and I slowly opened the door by backing away from the car.

When she stepped out of the car, I bowed down in front of her, tucking my right arm in and across my waist.

As she walked by me, she smacked the cowlick portion of my head with a swipe of her right hand, sending the hairs on the back of my head flying.

"Idiot," was all she said as she passed.

When she was about six feet away she turned back around to look at me. Her face was beet red, and she was laughing.

"How is it that you always manage to find some *stupid* new way to make me laugh!" she said.

"Because it's my only talent besides singing?" I said as a guess.

Karen had a lovely smile on her face as she walked back up to me and gave me a kiss. "Thanks for the ride, Wheezer. Catch up with ya after class?" she said.

"I'll be here!" I said.

I drove to the employee parking area to park and grabbed my work duffle bag out of the trunk of my car. I walked over to the locker room and changed from my street clothes into my work clothes. I stowed everything in my locker and headed out to the stage. I skipped the time clock, since I had no idea how this was all going to work. I was counting on Mike to perform his pen and eraser magic for me on my timecard.

There was plenty to do, and in no time at all I was lost in my work, even forgetting for a moment the amazing morning that I'd just had with Karen. It all still felt like a dream. And not to mention the fact that I'd still be taking her home tonight.

The shows kicked off on schedule, and Neil's set and the Carpenters show were both great. Karen looked terrific up there on stage. But I still tried to stay out of Karen's sight, however.

I realized that it was starting to become a superstitious obsession with me, as I became convinced that I had to do everything exactly the same way each night or I'd ruin the spell that I seemed to be under this week. Crazy I know, but when you don't understand a good thing when it keeps happening, these are the kind of explanations that you grasp at. I'm sure that gamblers understand exactly what I'm talking about.

But the reality was that it wasn't just staying the same. Each new day was *so* much better than the day before. But whatever it was, I sure didn't want to accidentally upset the karma.

As soon as her show was over I headed toward the locker room to take a shower. I knew that there were still things left to do around the stage, but for once in my life I left those for someone else to take care of.

After I dried off, I pulled a clean set of street clothes out of my bag and got dressed. I was just hoping that my calculations were correct, and that I had enough clothes packed for the whole weekend. I grabbed my bag and hurried out to my car, put the bag in my trunk, and drove over to the gate to wait for Karen.

After about 15 minutes Karen and a few others came out of the building. I saw her wave goodnight to the others as they walked off to their rides, and she headed over toward me.

If there was any doubt with the others about what was going on with Karen and me before, there certainly wasn't now. The only remaining confusion might be that Bear thought Danny's car was mine, and my car is white, not orange like his. But in any case, it was clear that Karen was with someone.

I met her at the passenger door, and she half ran up to me and gave me a kiss.

"Hi there, *you!*" she said.

"How was school?" I asked her.

She just smiled.

"Let me get the door for you, I know that you're not familiar with these 'merican cars," I said.

Karen just shook her head.

I don't think she was used to receiving as much busting as she usually dished out. She scooted over to be right next to me on the car seat for the ride back to the Inn.

Karen talked about something that had happened backstage before the show, which had her laughing so much she had trouble finishing the story! Once she was done she kept that sweet smile on her face for what little was left of the trip. Her left hand was resting on my thigh for the whole ride back, probably as a substitute for not being able to hold hands while I was driving. It was nice.

When we got to the Inn I parked in the same back lot area that I did before.

"Sorry for the long walk in," I said. "I hate door dings."

"No problem," Karen said with a smile.

I went around to the trunk and got my bag out.

"That's it?" Karen said.

"Yes. It should be everything I need. I didn't pack any evening clothes because you're working during the dinner hours. Did I screw up?" I said.

Karen just laughed. "No, it's not that. I'm so used to traveling on the road with crates full of clothes, I forgot what it's like to pack for a weekend! You should see the main one I have. The guys call it 'Blackula.' It's huge," she said.

We made our way into the hotel and up to the suite. When we got inside I put my bag down.

"I'm going to take a shower, but I won't be long," Karen said. "If you feel like some, why don't you pour us both a glass of wine while you're waiting. I'll be right back."

No sooner had I opened a bottle of wine and poured two glasses and brought them over to the sofa then Karen was back out again, dressed in her bath robe.

"Wow, you weren't kidding," I said. "That was fast."

"It's a lot easier when I don't have to do my hair," she said.

We settled down on the sofa. Karen was sitting right next to me, with her two legs tucked in on the sofa on the far side. Her right arm was around my neck holding my shoulder. We each took a sip of wine and put the glasses down, and she rested her head up against my arm and the sofa. We sat there for a few minutes like that, just sitting together.

"This is nice," I said.

There was no reply. I turned slightly to see that Karen had fallen asleep up against me. I just smiled. She had had a busy day; we both did. But then she had a show to do, too. I can't imagine the energy it must take to perform in front of thousands of people.

I just sat there for about 10 minutes, letting her sleep while I thought about the last 24 hours. What a great day it had been. Karen never made a sound or moved a muscle the entire time.

I turned, gave her a kiss on the forehead, and said, "Let's get you tucked into bed, Missy."

"Mmmm ..." was her only reply. I carefully picked her up and carried her into the bedroom. She never woke up.

I had a very restful night's sleep. I woke up slowly, almost as if I were fighting off the effects of a drug. When I finally opened my eyes, there was Karen, still asleep on the next pillow. She was on her side, facing me. I just laid there for a few minutes looking at every detail of her face. I even saw a freckle near her hairline that I'd never noticed before, just like the one below her eyebrow that was so cute.

After a few minutes she started making some waking up noises, mostly soft "Mmmm" moans. Her eyes opened slowly, and she saw me there on the next pillow, still looking at her. She smiled.

"Good morning, *you*," she said.

I smiled back. "Sleep ok?" I asked.

"Yes I had a *wonderful* night's sleep. But what happened last night? I can't remember a thing," she said.

"I'm not surprised, young lady," I said. "That was a whole flock of wine that you drank last night."

"I did?" she said.

"Yes, and where did you ever learn to dance like that?" I said.

Karen just squinted her eyes at me and said, "I think you're an even bigger buster than I am."

I just smiled.

"You fell asleep after one sip of wine," I said. "I had you tucked into bed not even 15 minutes after you came out of the shower."

"Oh, that hot shower must have just *knocked* me out. I'm sorry that I wasn't good company," she said.

"I enjoyed every minute," I replied.

"Thanks, Wheezer," she said with a smile.

"She's awake, folks!" I said.

Karen just grinned.

We had a very leisurely morning in our room. We ordered some breakfast and a large pot of coffee from room service. It was the first real breakfast that I'd had in days, between buttered rolls or skipping breakfast entirely. Karen just had some dry toast and coffee.

At one point Karen got up to retrieve some milk from the frig for another cup of coffee. As she walked into the kitchen, I couldn't help but check her out from behind (hey … I'm a guy), all the while thinking what a lucky sod I was to be here with her.

As she turned toward the frig to open the door, Karen caught me looking and just smiled. "I should think that you would be all caught up with that from Monday, when you were checking me out up on stage before the show," she said.

"Oh, Lord," I said, as I banged my forehead against the table, with my right arm cradling my head to hide it.

Karen had a huge smile of satisfaction on her face, and it was obvious that she had been saving that one all week, to bust me with it at just the right time.

"Smooth move, Captain Obvious," I said to myself out loud, as I lifted my head back up.

"No, you weren't obnoxious about it or anything. It was cute. The only reason I probably caught you is because I was checking you out now and then myself," she said.

"Who knows, it might even be the reason why you're here this morning. The start of it anyway," she said with a wink.

Just as she got back to our table with the milk, she gave my arm a squeeze before sitting down herself.

I was still feeling a bit embarrassed by having been caught — twice — and I said, "And here I was thinking all this time that it was my motorcycle. *That's* the reason why I thought you were attracted to me ... "

Karen just tilted her head and scrunched her forehead, not following what I was saying.

"You know, the whole 'bad boy' biker image? That motorcycle is like a g-spot with two wheels for some women," I said.

Karen just lifted up her eyebrows in surprise.

"So I've read ... but you know those 'Dear Penthouse' letters are probably *all* made up anyway," I added.

Karen just smiled and shook her head no as she took a sip of coffee. "You? A bad boy?" she said. "Give me a break!"

Once we were all done with breakfast I said, "So what are you in the mood for today? Anything special?"

"If it's ok, I'd really like to see the ocean again," she said. "I enjoyed it the other day. But somewhere new. Is there another place that we can go?"

"There are several," I said. "But I know just the spot. Bring along your magic hat, though, because it will be crowded."

Karen just smiled. "Always," she said.

She threw a few things into a shoulder bag for the trip. She also applied some sunscreen lotion just before we left, knowing that we'd be outside all day. I did as well.

We made our way out to the car and drove off.

"So where are we headed today?" she asked.

"The town is called Point Pleasant. There's a big boardwalk, a nice beach, and lots to see. It's a great spot for people watching," I said.

"Sounds perfect," she said.

After driving for about 45 minutes, we were there. I managed to luck out and find a parking spot only about a half block from the beach.

We headed over to the boardwalk and started exploring. Karen and I were holding hands as we walked along. We talked more about things we enjoyed, memories growing up, school, music — a little bit of everything really.

The beach was so wide here, just like Sandy Hook, and a lot of people were enjoying the day out at the shore. Lots of folks were out on the boardwalk: couples like us walking along, families, older folks sitting on benches watching the activity around them, and others just making their way to and from the beach. There were also plenty of arcade-type noises and music.

Karen's magic hat was working perfectly today, too. Every now and then as we were walking and talking, she'd turn up to look at me to make eye contact, but otherwise she kept her head down.

It was well after noon when we decided to grab a bite to eat. There was a waterfront restaurant that I had been to once before that I wanted to bring her to. Just a lovely setting, with great food, whether simple or fancy. I was wishing just then that we could be there together for dinner. It would have been very romantic by candlelight.

"So you know what to do, right?" I said to Karen.

"Yup, got it," she replied.

We walked into the restaurant entrance and we were soon greeted by the hostess. "Two for lunch today?" she asked.

"Yes, please," I said. "And I was wondering. Do you have a table with a water view, but something private?"

Just as I said this, Karen tilted her head up to look at the hostess, as I had asked her to. The hostess recognized Karen immediately, her eyes grew larger for a second, and she started to smile.

"We were hoping not to be disturbed," I added.

"Yes, of *course*," the hostess said. "Let me just check and I'll be *right* back."

It wasn't 30 seconds later that she returned with someone who I assumed was the owner.

"It's an honor to have you with us today," he said. "I have the perfect table for you. Please come with me."

Karen and I followed him to the water side of the restaurant and, as promised, he directed us to a nice corner table. She took the seat facing the water with her back to the room. I sat on the other side of the table, facing in toward the restaurant.

Just a few seconds later the owner returned and directed the two employees with him to remove the empty table and two chairs closest to us.

"For your comfort," he said with a smile. "Enjoy your lunch."

"I didn't mean to show you off," I said. "But I thought that you might get hounded here for autographs if we were seated just anywhere. I hope that I didn't embarrass you back there."

Karen just smiled, shaking her head. "No, it was a good idea," she said. "I usually don't mind an autograph or two, at least once I'm done eating! But I'd really like to just relax today. I decided that I'm officially on vacation this week. During the day, anyway. I need it bad."

She reached over and gave my hand a squeeze, and then she took off her floppy hat and placed it on the empty chair at our table.

She *did* look relaxed.

We checked out the menu and placed our order.

Each time they brought something out to our table — our drinks, warm rolls and butter, extra napkins, anything — it was a different server. Each one would place their item on the table, make eye contact with Karen, start smiling, and leave. I think they cycled through the entire waitstaff during our lunch, each of them getting a chance to "meet" Karen. She seemed amused by it all.

Lunch was delicious, and we even split a desert, with Karen trying a few tiny forkfuls. I asked for the check, and yet one last new young fellow brought it over, visibly nervous.

"Here you go," he said, his voice slightly trembling.

Karen and I smiled at each other once he had walked away. I paid for lunch and left a generous tip, feeling guilty now for having shown off Karen and probably costing the servers several tables worth of tips.

As we got up from the table to leave, Karen pulled her hat back on. When we reached the front of the restaurant, there was the owner and what looked like the entire staff, all standing in front of the wall alongside the door.

Karen happened to notice a camera sitting there on the counter, and she started to smile.

"Hey, do you think that we might have time for a group photo?" she said to them.

The owner and the others were all visibly thrilled. I'm sure that it was just what they were hoping for, but they were probably too embarrassed to ask.

Karen took off her hat and stood in the middle of the whole group.

I picked up the camera and said, "Ok, everyone ready?" Everyone smiled as I took the photo.

"Now one with just me and our host," Karen said, pulling the owner aside so that I could take a photo of just the two of them. He looked so happy.

"Please come again soon," he said, as we left.

Karen pulled her hat back on as we walked out of the restaurant, hoping to get away before any of the other patrons figured out what was happening.

"That was so sweet of you!" I said. "But I'm sorry you still had to work."

Karen just smiled, "I never really mind spending some time with nice people," she said. "It was a wonderful lunch. Thank you for bringing me here today."

She had the loveliest smile on her face. With that she reached up and gave me a kiss.

We continued walking along, eventually completing our round trip of the whole boardwalk.

"Let's head back," she said with a smile.

We got into the car and drove back to the Inn.

"Another perfect day," Karen said as we both sat down on the sofa in our room.

"I had a real nice time," I said, as I settled in next to her.

After a few minutes relaxing I became a little self-conscious, and I said, "You know what, I think I need to excuse myself for a few minutes and go take a shower and change into some fresh clothes. A little too much 'fun' at the beach today."

Karen just smiled and nodded as I grabbed my bag and brought it with me into the bedroom.

I pulled some fresh clothes out of my bag and placed them on the chair just outside the bathroom door. I then pulled out a few toiletries and went in to take a shower. The water was nice and warm, just as Karen had described. It was relaxing.

Once I was done, I toweled off and came out of the bathroom. I looked over at the chair, but the clothes that I had laid out there a few minutes ago were all gone.

It was then that I heard Karen say, "You don't need those just yet."

I looked up to see just her head poking out from under the bedcover, with an adorable smile on her face.

—

An hour or so later we were both dressed and headed off to the Arts Center for her show that night.

Other than when I was driving, we were almost always holding hands now. We talked on the ride in, but no serious topics, just whatever came into our heads. Mostly we both seemed content to just be in each other's company.

When we got to the Arts Center I dropped her off as usual. She gave me a nice kiss and got out of the car. It seems that she had used the trip today to study the door, and she finally located the handle, which blended in so seamlessly with the interior trim.

"Later!" she said with a smile, as she turned to walk into the building.

I parked my car and went in to change into my work clothes. The evening flew by quickly. I only saw my boss, Mike, once as he walked by the section of stage I was working. Other than smiling and nodding slightly, he never slowed down.

In no time at all the show was over and I showered yet again. I just put my clothes back on from the trip over, since they were only an hour old.

I pulled up to the artists' gate section to wait for Karen. When I saw her headed my way, I got out of the car to open the door for her. She smiled and said, "Hi" in her usual fashion, and got in, but something seemed off tonight. I started to wonder if she was getting grief from anyone for seeing me.

I headed back toward the Inn, letting her sit for awhile with her thoughts. She was still sitting right up next to me, with her hand on my leg, so I was thankful for that part.

After a few more minutes of silence, I said, "Do you want to talk about it?"

Karen looked over toward me and put on a partial smile, but she just shook her head no and turned back to look straight ahead, saying nothing for the rest of the trip.

We pulled into the Inn parking lot and I parked the car. We both got out and headed toward the lobby. She reached for my hand immediately as we walked. I still had no idea what was on her mind. We took the elevator up to the suite, and I opened the door.

Before I could even turn on the light, Karen came up to me, put her arms around me, and said, "Just hold me, ok?"

I let the room door swing closed behind us. We stood like that for several minutes in the dark, while she had the side of her head resting up against my chest.

Just then she turned her head back toward me, gave me a kiss, and whispered, "Let's go to bed."

# Sunday, August 10, 1975

I woke up Sunday morning with the sun just peeking onto my pillow through the side edge of one of the blinds on the windows. I looked around the room to see that I was all alone. I had just had the most peaceful night's sleep of my life. It's hard to describe. The nearest other experience I've ever known was when I had some minor surgery, and they gave me an intravenous drug of some type and said to start counting back from one hundred. I remember getting to about 94.

But last night was such a deep restful sleep, with no tossing and turning, no waking up five times during the night, no invasive dreams — no dreams at all that I could recall. I woke up completely renewed. I went into the bathroom to freshen up for a minute, and then I went out to search for Karen.

I caught sight of her sitting out on the balcony in her robe, one leg over the other, swinging away. She was drinking a cup of coffee and playing with her hair, just enjoying the morning. I went out onto the balcony and came up from behind her. Just as I reached her she turned her head up and back to look at me and lifted her left forearm up to brush my arm. I cupped the side of her chin with my own hand from behind and gave her a kiss on the top of the head, right at the line between her hair and her forehead. Her hair smelled so good.

"Hey, good morning, *you*," she said with a smile.

"Hiya," I said as I smiled back.

"You looked so peaceful in there sleeping that I didn't want to disturb you, so I closed the bedroom door and came out here," Karen said.

"Thanks for that. I did have a great night's sleep," I said.

"I made some coffee. Why don't you grab a cup and come join me," she said.

"I will, thanks," I replied. I let my hand kinda slide up her still raised forearm, until I got to her hand. I gave that a squeeze and said, "Be right back."

Karen seemed her normal self this morning, so I was still not sure what last night was all about. I didn't plan to bring it up just now, because whatever it was, she seemed to be at peace with it.

After a few minutes I rejoined Karen outside on the balcony, taking the chair next to hers. I set my coffee down on the small table between our two chairs.

"What a great morning," she said with a smile, looking over toward me as she spoke.

I smiled and nodded. We sat there, just enjoying the breeze.

"I think we might get a little rain later," I said, after feeling a sudden strong gust of wind out of nowhere. But for now the sky was bright, with only a few clouds.

"Is that your 'motorcycle experience' talking?" she smiled.

"I *do* hate to get wet," I said, nodding.

As we sat there for a few minutes I suddenly became curious about something, so I turned to Karen and said, "Can I ask you something a little personal?"

She turned her head toward me with a smile, kinda opening up her two hands resting on the arms of her chair. She looked down and around herself, like "Dude, I'm falling out of my robe here after being locked in a hotel room with you for two days. What's more personal?"

I smiled back, "No, it's not like that. I don't actually know why I'm embarrassed to ask you this," I said.

Karen gave me a mischievous look and said, "I'm not doing a 3-way if that's what you're thinking," she snickered.

"Oh, quit it," I said with a laugh.

Then I paused and slowly rolled my eyes up and to one side, as though I were considering what she had just said.

Karen gave my arm a slap and said, "Now *you* quit it! What!" she asked.

"It just occurred to me. Do you ever get tired of singing the same songs every night at your shows? I mean, I know that's what the people come for. But I was just wondering how *you* feel about it," I said.

Karen turned back to look at the view for a minute as she considered the question, and then took another sip of coffee.

After a moment she turned back toward me and said, "That's not a yes or no question, I can tell you that much.

It's a lot more subtle than that. I can see how you might wonder about it, though. How many times have I sung 'Close to You,' a thousand times? Ten thousand times? I don't really know. Maybe I don't really *wanna* know," she said with a chuckle.

"But think of it this way ..." she started to say.

Just then I got a huge smile on my face.

"*What?!*" she said, mid-sentence.

"You're starting to sound like me!" I said.

Karen got a huge blush on her face, realizing that I was a little bit right.

After a second or two she continued, "Anyway ... what was I saying before I was so *rudely* interrupted?" She smiled. "Oh yes. Think of it this way. Everyone goes off to work each day. On a good day maybe you don't mind. On bad days you dread it. Whatever the job — in an office, on an assembly line, even baking apple pies. But you go.

"In that way, my 'job' is not a lot different than anyone else's. People assume that just because there are more zeros on my paycheck, that I must get bored a lot faster.

"But when you get up there in front of a thousand smiling faces, all applauding just at the sight of you, it *is* a little different. These people have so many happy memories wrapped up in your songs. You feel that energy, and you feed on it. It makes *you* feel good to make *them* feel good by singing these songs for them.

"Maybe that's one reason why I'm such a fussbudget about always having our stage show sound exactly like the recordings, as much as possible, I mean. Because I know that any unexpected change is going to spoil that moment for a lot of people," she said.

"Believe me, I've blasted a few of the guys for fooling around too much on stage during a show," she added.

"I never even considered any of this. But you're right, it probably would," I said.

"Once or twice a year we might have a dud show, where we never connect with the audience," she said. "But those are really the exception. I can never figure those nights out. We all look around at each other at the end of the show and wonder, 'What happened? What did we do wrong?'"

"But in answer to your question, do I always feel like it?" she said. "No, not always. But I don't usually mind. But if I ever stopped feeling good about it, and just started dreading doing each song one more time, night after night, then no ... That would be the day I'd quit," she added. "But that's just me. I don't know how other artists feel."

We sat there quietly after this for a few minutes, and I was just thinking about everything that she had said. She was so articulate.

Karen looked like she was thinking about something, too, but I still wasn't sure what. Was it last night again? She was unusually fidgety, and she was still playing with her hair like before — just curling it around her one finger, over and over, on the side of her head — something that I'd never seen her do before.

It was just then that she turned to me and said, "Actually, I should thank you for breaking the ice a little bit with your personal question. I kinda have a personal question for you, too, that I have been hesitating to bring up this morning."

I looked over to study Karen's face just then because she sounded very serious. I sure didn't think that any kind of joke was in order.

"What is it Karen? You have me a bit concerned," I said.

"Oh, it's not a bad thing, I don't think. At least I hope not. And if I'm *way* out of line here, just tell me so. I'll understand," she said.

I just kept looking at her, searching for a clue as to what was coming.

"Well, I was just thinking that we'll be wrapping up our tour in a few more weeks," she said. "I know that you're headed off to school yourself next month. But I wanted to run a crazy idea by you. What would you say to switching schools and coming to study out in California, maybe at Cal State, near me?

"By the time you get settled into your new routine with the move and classes and all, I'd already be back. I mean you're going out of state anyway for school, so I didn't think that this move would be any bigger a disruption for you, would it?" she said. "We'd have some time together before I head overseas — and you'll have your studies to focus on while I'm gone anyway. So I'd really be back in no time."

As she spoke, Karen started to feel a bit more comfortable with her thoughts. "And think about it. I'm going to have that big new apartment there soon. It would be great to have you over. You'd be so helpful with the decorating! Maybe you could stay over now and then and we can take some long weekend trips. Or even move in, I mean, if you ever wanted to … *someday*."

Karen started to feel embarrassed now, like perhaps she had gone too far in her excitement, wondering if I might be feeling trapped. She stopped talking just then to look for my reaction, and to hear what I was thinking.

"Karen, I'll be honest with you. These last few days — really this whole week since I met you — it's been the first time in my life that I wasn't thinking for one minute about tomorrow. I was just enjoying my time with you. I knew that your last day here would be coming soon enough. I didn't want to waste one second of my time with you worrying about it.

"Now that I think about it, I'm actually surprised that the whole thing didn't keep me up all night last night, this being your last day here and all. I usually have no control over my dreams," I said.

"But, yes, what you're saying sounds really good. Wonderful even! I think that it could work out perfectly," I replied.

Karen was thrilled. "Oh, I'm so glad you agree! I really thought it made sense. Other than a short while yesterday, I wasn't thinking too much about the future for the same reason as you. I didn't want this moment to end. But then I realized last night that maybe it doesn't have to."

Karen was almost giddy as she spoke.

But now I understood what had happened last night.

Karen continued, "I was thinking about it and I started to wonder if this was just the craziest idea I've ever had. I've never done anything this spontaneous before. It goes against all the rules in my book. But I don't care! I'm tired of wasting time waiting. I don't even know what I'm waiting for anymore! My own damn rules are keeping me from enjoying my own *life*," she said.

"You've got rules?" I asked.

"Rules, yes. And checklists," she said.

"Of your perfect guy, or something else?" I said.

"Yes ... well, my wishlist anyway. That and for a lot of other things, too," she said.

"That's my Karen," I said smiling, "Always looking for perfection in an imperfect world!"

"I know that I'm a crazy perfectionist sometimes," she said. "But I don't care! Is that so bad?"

I just smiled and said, "No, I don't think it's so bad. But tell me something, in all honesty. How many of these check boxes do I really satisfy?"

A little more serious this time, she replied, "The most important ones."

I started nodding my head as I heard this, understanding what this might be about.

"Karen, I know that I'm not rich and famous and probably never will be. But I hope you understand that I don't give a darn about those things. It really doesn't matter that much to me. You could quit singing tomorrow and start giving out flowers at the airport, and I wouldn't care. But I'd never ask you to quit because I know you love it. It's your life.

"We all need money to get by, but it's not my measure of success in life. The richest person may be the most unhappy of all. Most of all, I just want to be happy," I said.

"Oh, I know that, silly. It never crossed my mind," she said.

"Well, I'm glad," I said. "You told me yourself the other day, that deep down inside you're just a regular person, too. So we're really just two 'regular people'."

Karen nodded.

"And it just so happens that one of us is incredibly talented, while the other of us is only incredibly *handsome* — and sings like Alfalfa," I said.

Karen let out a surprised chuckle.

She sprang up from her chair, sat in my lap, and threw her arms around my neck. "Then it's all settled. Oh, I'm so glad!"

She reached in to give me a quick kiss and got right back up and ran into the kitchen, carrying our two empty coffee mugs to the sink.

"No running in the house," I teased.

I actually heard Karen giggle like a schoolgirl from the kitchen. I followed her in.

"Oh, I'm so happy! You'll see, you'll be happy too!" she said.

I smiled and said, "You already make me happy."

Karen smiled. "I'm going to hop in and take a quick shower. But I'll be back in a little bit," she said.

As she rushed off I said, "Maybe I'll join you in there in a few minutes!"

I could hear Karen giggle again from the bathroom. She was downright giddy. I was so happy, too.

Just as I was standing there thinking about all this, a feeling of dread came over me. The smile faded away from my face. I sat down in the chair and my mind was soon swimming with intrusive thoughts. I suddenly got very depressed.

I lost all track of time while Karen was away, as my head was spinning with these thoughts.

A short while later, Karen came out of the bathroom wearing a white terrycloth robe and her slippers, and she had a small white towel wrapped around her wet hair, in the shape of a small bun.

"What happened to you? I thought you were coming in to join me. Did you change your mind?" she said.

She stood there in front of me with a lovely smile on her face. Her body had the scent of warm vanilla.

"I'm perfectly spotless," she said. "Come on …" as she reached for my hands to pull me up out of the chair, "Let's go into the other room."

After a few seconds her smile started to fade as she stood there looking at me, when I didn't get up and I didn't respond.

She suddenly let go of both my hands, and said, "What's going on?"

"Karen, I can't do this. I can't move to California. I don't know what I was thinking before," I said.

As I said these words, a look of horror came over Karen's face. She took it all in for a few more seconds, and then turned and frantically reached for the end table drawer, pulling out a cigarette and some matches from inside. Her hands were trembling so much that she could hardly light it.

"Twenty minutes ago, you said it was wonderful. That you were so happy. That it was perfect. What changed? I didn't change! Tell me!" she said.

"I just know that it would be a big mistake, believe me …" I said.

Karen just stood there for a minute staring at me. Suddenly the look of horror on her face was replaced with one of anger. She stood more erect, as though suddenly charged with electricity.

"What … so you were just stringing me along before, thinking that you'd knock out another quickie before you go? Is that it? Did you chicken out? What's really going on here?" she said.

After a short pause she added, "Oh, my God! This whole weekend has been some kind of hump & dump shipboard fling for you, without the ship. Is there even a *word* for it? "Man, your buddy Danny sure could learn a thing or *two* from you!"

She was furious.

"Karen, you couldn't be more wrong," I said. "That's not what this is about."

"Well, you'd better hurry up and tell me what the *hell* this is all about, then, because I'm starting to feel cheap and used," she said, as she took another long drag on her cigarette.

"Karen, I believe I'm falling in love with you," I said. "I'm sure of it, actually. But it was *you* who seduced *my* mind. And you were right... everything else followed willingly."

Upon hearing those words, Karen froze in place and just stared at me, unblinking. But I could tell that all the stress built up in her body from the last two minutes was escaping from her chest in one long exhale.

I reached up and took her hand. "Please ..." I said, as I motioned for her to sit down on the chair next to me. She did, but her body seemed rigid, as though frozen in shock. She sat on the very edge of the cushion.

"Karen, all those wonderful plans were a dream come true for me. You were offering me the whole world, but the only part of it that I really wanted or cared about was you. And for a moment I was caught up in the fantasy. But while you were in the shower, reality crept back in. I realized that there was no way you'd ever really be happy with me. Not in the end. I'm damaged goods. And I know that once you figured that out, it would be the end of our relationship.

"But I also realized something else. I realized that I love you. And I knew that I couldn't bear the pain of losing you. Of having the best thing that I've ever found in my life taken away from me, just like every other joy I've ever known. As bad as today is for me, that day would be a hundred times worse," I said.

"There are some things that you don't know about me. Remember that story I was telling you the other day, about the girl and the crystal?" I said.

"The girl you knew all your life," Karen said.

"Yes. She lived right next door to me. We were the two oldest kids on the block. Michelle and I used to play all types of games together every day for over a year. One day she just disappeared. I was a 4-year-old kid whose whole world was suddenly gone. No one knew that I was panicking for days over this. I couldn't figure out what I did for her to leave," I said.

"She had started school. It was only years later I learned that her parents wouldn't let her play with me on the weekends or even after school anymore, either, so she wouldn't miss me during the week. I realized years later that what should have been a normal childhood adjustment probably scarred that 4-year-old kid for life," I said.

205

"Or my very first school crush in the fourth grade, Joanne. We walked home from school together every day. She made me a Valentine's Day card. One day the school principal came and took her out of class, and I never saw her again. Our teacher told us the next week that her father had been killed in a car accident, and her mother took her and moved back with her family. Everyone I ever cared about kept leaving me.

"You think that you can just say 'big deal, get over it,' but if everything in life was that simple, then no one would ever have any issues. But it's not.

"And the other story about my Dad and me fishing once, but never again?" I said.

"Yes," she replied.

"As much as I wanted to do it again each year, I never asked. Do you know why? Because I was more afraid of learning that my own father didn't want to spend time with me than of anything. That perhaps I'd embarrassed him somehow by my behavior on the boat that one trip, by being too silly because I was happy. I never saw him except for weekends. No matter what I tried, it seemed to take me all of five minutes to make him angry when I was with him. I could never do or say the right thing. Finally, I just stayed away from him as much as I could. The only time I could truly relax was when I was away from home," I said.

"One day, years before that, when I was about 7, I came home from school and my father had bought a small model ship for us to put together. We spent two hours doing that before he went to work. I was so happy. It sat on top of the china cabinet for years. But we never did it again. For years afterward my pace would quicken on the walk home from grade school when I wondered if today might be the day that there would be another model waiting for me — along with my Dad — when I got home. But there never was," I said.

"For my 13th birthday my Dad unexpectedly loaded me into our 1957 Chevy, and the two of us drove down to Asbury Park together. We listened to the car radio, we talked, we walked the boardwalk, and we played pinball. I was in heaven. But we never did it again. We never even spoke of it.

"I was older by this point, and I was starting to wonder if that's as much as anyone could tolerate of me. That maybe the only reason he did it in the first place was because my mother was nagging him to not ignore me," I said.

"My self-esteem never got fed, only my insecurities. I didn't have any explanations, so I filled in my own. 'This is what happiness feels like. What? You want more? You're not worth it.' Even that stupid car of mine is just there to paper over my insecurities.

"In my whole life, my father told me he loved me exactly one time. And I was so stunned that I don't even remember if I said it back, if I said thank you, or if I said nothing at all. Deep down I think he must, but I have had a lifetime of never really knowing if he even liked me or was proud of me, never mind loved me.

"And I don't say these things to point blame at anyone else. I'm sure that he was doing the best that he knew how. All I'm saying is that little kid needed more. And now I'm left to try and unravel this wreck that I've turned myself into," I said.

"Karen, the other day you talked about feeling worthless sometimes? Well, I feel unlovable. I feel that whatever love comes my way is only because I've tricked someone into thinking that I was a normal person. And now I've tricked you. But once people realize how flawed I really am, they'll abandon me. I think it's why I'm so thin-skinned with criticism, and why I try to do everything to perfection in life: to prove to myself and to everyone else that I'm not 'really' all that bad. Or why my brain never shuts off, because I've spent my entire life trying to understand what was wrong with me, and why I didn't deserve to feel joy for more than a few minutes at a time, every couple of years, with nothing but anger waiting for me in between, it seemed. I put on a good act, but inside I'm just scared as hell," I said.

"So now you can see that I know a little bit about your situation. We're both broken people, Karen. That's why I can't move to California with you. There is no way that I could ever give you the support that you deserve. I can't even help myself yet.

"I hope one day we can both sort out our lives. And I just know that if I ever do, I'm coming back to find you just as fast as I can, hoping that I'm not too late. And it kills me to believe that this is the only way we might ever be happy together, because now that I've known your touch, I know *exactly* what I'm giving up," I said.

I stopped talking just then, feeling very self-conscious about having rambled on for so long. I had just snapped under the emotional strain, just like Karen did the other day.

All this time she listened to everything I said, sensing that it would be good for me to get it all out of my system, perhaps for the first time in my life.

After a moment she stood up and came over to me, sat in my lap, and put her left arm around my neck and shoulder. She kissed me softly on the forehead, and just stroked my temple with her other hand as she pulled my head over toward her chest and shoulder.

"Shhh," she said. "I understand."

We sat there for a long time, almost tangled up around each other in that chair. The whole time Karen continued softly stroking the side of my face.

I'd lost all track of time by the point I heard her say, "Tell me about that one time."

I turned to look at her and said, "My father?"

Karen nodded.

"I was around 11 years old. That summer my grandmother decided that she wanted to go back to Europe to visit all the friends and family that she left behind years ago to come here, and maybe see the old family farm one more time. She offered to bring me with her on the trip. When the day finally came to leave, my father drove us to the airport for the flight. We had so many suitcases that there was no room in the car for anyone else.

"Those were the days before jetways and safety rules, when passengers still had to walk out onto the tarmac to their planes and climb up a long set of metal stairs to get into the aircraft. My father accompanied us all the way to the fence, just 100 feet from the plane. You could still do that back then. My grandmother said her goodbyes to my father, as did I, and we both turned to board the plane.

"I only got about two steps away when I heard my father say 'Johnny.' I turned back around. He said, 'I forgot something.' I walked back over to him. It was then that he gave me a big hug. I could feel the five o'clock shadow of his beard as he pressed his cheek up against mine. He said, 'I love you'. I don't know what I did. Maybe I nodded. I hurried away to catch up to my grandmother," I said.

"They called you Johnny back then?" she asked.

"Only my parents. They still do to this day. It's actually the name on my birth certificate," I said.

Karen just smiled. "So instead of a million 'I love yous' over the course of a lifetime that you probably wouldn't remember, you got just one 'I love you' that you never forgot."

I nodded yes.

Karen sat quietly for a long time, just thinking, it seems, but still stroking my forehead. I found it comforting. Just then she stood up to face me in the chair. She raised both arms toward me palm sides up, with her fingers motioning for me to come here. She had a lovely smile on her face.

"Come ... let's go lie down in the other room for a while," she said.

I took her hand and followed her away.

—

It was getting to be late in the afternoon when we both found ourselves sitting next to each other at the small dinette table in the kitchen, sipping coffee. There was no more conversation other than the most basic. The mood became more somber as we both understood that our week together was finally over. We had simply run out of time.

It was then that Karen turned to me and softly said, "I'm going to ride into the Arts Center with the guys this afternoon, ok?"

I didn't really react. I just let that sink in for a minute.

Without even looking at her, I finally said, "Wow, it really is real now, isn't it?"

She reached out for my forearm with her hand and gave it a squeeze. I turned to look at her.

She started shaking her head. "No, it's not that. I want you to come back and meet me at the gate tonight after the show, one more time," she said. After a short pause she added, "But bring your motorcycle."

I squeezed her hand and smiled. She smiled back.

"I'm gonna go and get ready for the show, while you drive back home and get your bike. But I'll see you later tonight, ok?" she said.

After a few seconds, she got up, kissed me one more time, and then turned to go into the bedroom. I thought about all of this for a moment, got up to pack a few of my things into my bag, and I left.

For the whole drive home, all I did was think about Karen and our time together the last few days. That was the only thing I cared about. It did finally rain for a short while during the drive back, but the storm blew by quickly. The roads dried up in no time once the sun returned.

I got home in short order, went inside, and put my bag on my bed. I stripped down and headed straight into the shower. I felt like I was in there for a half hour. The hot water felt comforting somehow, and I wanted all the comforting I could get just then. I stood there and let the hot water just wash down over my face and body.

After I dried off, I put on some fresh clothes and, after a little more grooming, I started rooting around in my closet for a second jacket and a passenger helmet. I brought all of this out to my bike and strapped it all onto the back of the seat.

A quick check of the bike's gas tanks showed that I was low, so I grabbed the five-gallon can from the back of the garage and topped off both tanks. I didn't know where we were going tonight, but I knew that I wasn't going to spend one minute of our time together in a gas station. I zipped up my leather jacket, put on my helmet, and got the bike going.

A few minutes later I was headed toward the Arts Center. I didn't allow myself to think about this evening on the ride there, or to wonder about what might happen later. Whatever it was, I wanted to experience it live and fresh, like it was a new movie that I had never seen before.

I didn't know if this was a good idea or not, but I suddenly had a strong desire to try and do things differently in my life, thinking that perhaps this might help give me the fresh start that I wanted.

I got to the Arts Center parking lot and parked in my normal spot. I walked the short distance to my locker and stashed my gear. I wouldn't need it for a few hours, not until after the show.

I felt guilty about it, but I had no energy left to help out backstage tonight. I hoped that Mike was serious about that comment to work if I could.

Soon I heard Neil Sedaka start his performance. I went out toward the stage to settle in. No disrespect to Neil, but I'm afraid that I was lost to my own thoughts through his whole show, and it was soon over.

It was then that I saw Karen walk out on stage, and my heart seemed to stop. I looked around for a place to stand where I could be invisible. I found myself almost hugging the column that I was standing behind. I saw only enough of the stage to see Karen. I didn't need to see anything more.

I was glad that I was in the shadow of that column, because my face wasn't dry for a lot of the show. I watched every second of her on stage, but I could not tell you about one moment of her performance. The memory machine in my head was off tonight. Perhaps I finally broke it.

After Karen was done with her show, I snapped back to reality and walked over to my locker to get my gear. I also scrubbed my face with soap and water. I felt better, even if my red eyes probably betrayed my evening.

I had no idea what she was thinking of for tonight, but I didn't care how early I might be or how long I might wait. I got my bike and rode over to the gate to wait for her.

I wasn't there 10 minutes before I saw a solitary figure head up the path toward me from the stage area. I don't know what she did differently to get done faster, but I didn't care. She walked straight up to me and put her hand around the back of my neck to pull me in close. But it was not for a kiss, however. She brought me forward until our foreheads finally touched, and we stayed like that for a moment — she with her eyes closed.

Finally, she said, "Thank you for coming," and she gave me a soft kiss.

She looked down at the bike as though she were trying to figure out what to do.

I gave her my black leather jacket and said, "Put this on. You'll be warmer."

I put on the spare cloth jacket. I buckled the shorty helmet onto her head first and then I put on my own. I quickly started up the bike and got on. Karen was looking at me, and I nodded. She climbed on. She threw her arms around me tight, and I pulled away.

It was at this point I heard a voice yelling, "Karen!" I didn't know if someone was searching for her, or if they knew exactly where she was on the back of my bike. I didn't look back to find out.

I had no idea where we were going, but I instinctively headed toward the ocean and then south. We were soon cruising along the coast road along the Atlantic. It was a quiet Sunday night, and there was little traffic to slow us down. It was about an hour later that we got to our destination, Seaside Heights.

There was a large amusement pier with plenty of lights and noise and people, a roller coaster, and a ferris wheel. I tied all the gear to the bike, and Karen pulled her ever-present floppy hat out of her pocket and put it on. We slowly made our way to the boardwalk. Karen was holding my hand tight.

As we walked along the water side of the boardwalk, the lights and noise of the rides provided the background music for the evening. Neither one of us had said a word this entire time, not since Karen had thanked me for coming. But no words seemed necessary. All the good things had already been said, and we didn't want to talk about the rest.

We walked along slowly, with Karen holding on so tightly that she was almost transferring some of her own weight over to me. It wasn't even walking or strolling. It was so slow that I'm not sure that it has a name. We walked like this for almost an hour, until we reached the very end of the amusement part of the boardwalk.

We stopped at the very last railing and turned toward the water. It was too dark to see the ocean, but we could hear the surf hitting the shore. I put my right arm around her and pulled her in close. We stayed like this for a long time, still silent.

I don't know how long we stood there just listening to the sounds of the ocean, but at one point I took her hand and turned her toward me. I gave her a long hug. We held each other tight. We then started walking back.

I'm not sure why, but I found myself in front of the ferris wheel and, without thinking, I got two tickets. We both got on. I don't know if there were no other passengers or the fellow operating it just liked us, but the ride seemed to go on forever.

We stopped twice at the very top. After a few more turns it was time to get off. We resumed our slow walk back to where we began. All this time we were still holding hands.

When we got to the steps to leave the boardwalk, I just turned to Karen and smiled. She smiled back and gave my hand a squeeze. We walked back to the bike, put our riding gear back on, and we headed north. She had her hands in my jacket pockets as she held me tight for the whole ride back.

It was almost 4 AM by the time we pulled into the parking lot of the Holiday Inn. I killed my headlight as soon as I hit the lot and parked several rows away from the main entrance and off to one side, partially in the shadows. I didn't want our last few minutes together to be interrupted.

I turned off the engine, and we both got off the bike. I removed my helmet, while Karen took off her jacket and helmet and handed them back to me. I placed everything on the seat. We walked out in front of my bike, but this was as far as I would follow her.

Karen looked at me and placed her hand behind my neck.

As she did this I started to get choked up, and I tried to speak. "Karen, I ..." was all I could say before she started shaking her head slowly from side to side.

"I know …" was all she said, as the tears started to well up in her eyes. She reached in to give me one final kiss, and then she turned and quietly walked away toward the hotel.

I couldn't bear to watch her leave, so I turned back around toward my bike with my head hanging low. I just stood there for a moment, already wondering what I had just done.

I felt completely numb. I couldn't even breathe.

It was just then that I heard Karen's voice gently say, "Johnny."

I turned back around, and she was standing there right behind me.

"I forgot something," she said.

With that she wrapped her arms around me, pressing her cheek up against mine, and she whispered into my ear, "I love you."

Once she finished her long hug, Karen looked up at me one last time, looked back down, and then turned around to leave. This time I just stood there and watched as she walked over to the hotel.

When she reached the lighted overhang of the hotel in front of the main door, someone rushed out of the lobby toward her and started to speak. Karen's arm went straight out toward them, with her palm facing them.

"Don't!" is all she said, as she walked right by, barely even turning her head to look at them. Her arm finally swung back down to pull open the entrance door, and she walked straight into the hotel.

That person stood there for a few seconds, watching her walk away, and then turned back toward me. They stood there for a moment, just staring. I stood there motionless, leaning against my bike, just staring back. After another minute, they turned and went back into the hotel.

After all of this, I don't know how I didn't break down right then and there in the parking lot. I was probably still in shock from the whole experience, much like having a severe cut, but somehow not yet feeling the pain.

I tied down the spare jacket and helmet to the seat and I put on my own helmet and leather jacket to leave. It was just then that I noticed the scent of vanilla still on my jacket, from Karen having worn it.

I started the bike and headed home.

I was counting on the ride back to clear out the clutter in my mind. It was a jumble of wonderful memories, but also of instant regrets, doubts, and second guesses. And, thank God, after a few miles, a sudden feeling of calm did wash over me.

But this time it wasn't because my problems had been blown away by the ride. It was because I had just come to appreciate the last gift that Karen had just given me.

She understood, as perhaps no one else could, that the reason I loved my bike so much was because it was the one source of joy that I had found in my life that someone else couldn't take away. The pleasure it gave me is the same pleasure that Karen felt when she performed.

We had each found our own substitute for the love that was missing in our lives.

I think that she wanted me to have both of these joys — my bike, with her on back — together at the same time, even if it was only for a few hours.

And she was so right. She had given me so many wonderful new memories.

And it was all done without saying a single word.

# It's Really Real

After all of about three hours of sleep, I walked into Mike's office rather early on Monday morning and half slumped down into the chair in front of his desk. I looked up a second later to find him studying my face and body language, as he tried to piece together the answer to the question that was on his and everyone else's mind: "What happened with you and Karen?"

"I wasn't really sure if I'd be seeing you here today or not, John," Mike said.

I looked up at him and said, "Mike, if I had half a brain in my head, I wouldn't be here right now. Do you know that Karen asked me to move out to California to be with her?"

Mike thought about this for a minute. "So you weren't kidding the other day when you said that you two were crazy about each other, were you?" he said.

I just shook my head no.

"I thought you were besotted, yes. Who wouldn't be? But I didn't consider for a minute that it might be more than that," he said.

"Well, you're half right Mike. I *was* besotted last Wednesday. By Sunday, I was in love. We both were," I said.

Mike looked at me and said, "Do you know that she stopped by here on Friday to thank me for letting you have some time off. She looked like she was positively glowing with happiness. Now I understand why."

"Oh, I'm so glad that she did. She told me she planned to. Mike, she's the most beautiful, smart, sexy, and funny woman I've ever met in my life. She was my dream come true — any mans dream come true. And she offered me a world of happiness. And, basically, I was too afraid to say yes," I said.

After a moment, Mike replied, "I know you pretty well, John, and I just don't see how that could be true. You deserve to be happy, just as much as she does."

I looked up at him for a second. "Maybe … the only thing on my mind was that I didn't deserve this wonderful person, because I was afraid that I'd end up hurting her. I did hurt her a little bit you know, early last week, by being a fool. I never wanted to do that again," I said.

"I still think you're being too hard on yourself," Mike said. "You must have been doing a *whole* lot of things right to have the week that you just had with her. And after all that, for her to want you to come out to California to be with her … That's not nothing."

After a moment I nodded my head. "That's true, of course. I need to turn my head around about this and a whole lot of other things and stop being the victim in my own life. I'm wasting too much time. I'm wasting opportunities.

"Right now, the only thing on my mind is figuring out a way to be worthy to get her back someday and hoping that she'll still want me when I do," I said.

"Well, I hope you get it all sorted out," Mike said.

"Thanks, Mike. Well, I'd better get to work, I guess," I said.

As I stood up, I paused to say, "Please don't tell anyone what I just told you. I kinda just needed to get it off my chest. You already knew more of the story than anyone else. That and I trust you."

"I'll take it with me to my grave," he said.

"Oh, and ..." I started to say, before Mike interrupted me.

"Your timecard from last week went up to the front office last night. There's nothing to discuss," he said.

I half smiled, nodded a thank you, and left.

I got out to the stage area to get to work. I'd never been here this early on a Monday morning in the past to see what happened in the hours before the new acts came in. This week it would be Henry Mancini.

The Carpenters had already moved on to their next gig, which was in Colombia, Maryland, for the week. Most of the group were well on their way there, or already there, I was sure, since it was only a few hours south.

So the one thing that I knew for certain was that I wouldn't be seeing Karen's smiling face coming up to surprise me with a visit again or for her to find yet another new way to bust my chops. She was really gone. I missed her something awful.

I expected that work might not be very satisfying for me anymore, and I wasn't wrong. I still did everything to the best of my abilities, just like before, but in reality I was just going through the motions. I wasn't really sad or depressed. Mostly I was still numb. Time just seemed to stop for me. I sure wasn't the lighthearted kid that I had been just a week ago.

That's when I realized that I had built a wall around my heart a long time ago to make sure I stayed lighthearted. I didn't want anyone to ever hurt me. I was so tired of being hurt. But Karen had charmed her way in with her personality and her smile, and now everything had changed. But even with the heartache, I thought that this was still a positive thing. My idea to hide from love was not really a healthy life plan.

And speaking of changes, I was surprised by how I was being treated at work all of a sudden, too. Nothing bad or cruel, just different.

It occurred to me that this might have been what I was already starting to notice last week, when folks started acting weird, or Danny's strange comment that one morning. That was just as things started to get serious between me and Karen.

In their eyes, I *was* different.

I've had the experience later in life of going from staff to management, and it's a little bit like this, only *much* more so. Your friends suddenly don't feel comfortable teasing you like before. When you show up at the water cooler, they're a little more likely to leave than to share the gossip or TV show that they were just discussing.

Suddenly, here at work, I was no longer viewed as one of them. I certainly wasn't a celebrity, but I was no longer just John the stage crew guy either. I was something in between.

Mostly it felt like I was being shunned.

Even my best friend, Danny, was polite but never busting my chops at all anymore. There was never another music quiz that summer. And he never *once* asked me a single question about Karen or what had happened that week.

Did he think that he was doing me a kindness by not reminding me of her? I don't know. But I'm ashamed to say that as the weeks passed I became a little resentful that he never did ask. And this may have been the beginning of why we eventually drifted apart a year or two later.

During my last few weeks at the Arts Center, this treatment by everyone never changed. So I knew then that it was no temporary thing just to let me recover.

When I entered Karen's world, it seemed as though I had completely left my old world behind.

It was at this point that I decided that I would never tell anyone about my time with her. I didn't want other people acting weird around me, if this was the reaction that I'd get. And there was no scenario that I could think of to bring it up, anyway, where it didn't sound like bragging — and I despise braggarts.

And so it remained. Even after I left for college a few weeks later, or for many years to come, I never told a single soul about Karen.

The rest of August flew by very quickly because there was a lot to do before heading off to school. I sold my Lincoln about a week after Karen left. It had nothing to do with her. The deal was already in the works before I met her.

It certainly wasn't a practical car to have at school for the next four years. And in my talk with her on our last day together, I now understood that I also shouldn't use expensive toys to mask my insecurities.

But I realized something else: that deep down, I already *knew* this, but somehow I was denying or ignoring it. This admission to her wouldn't have just fallen out of my mouth. It was already a fully formed thought, but one that I had never admitted to myself.

What *else* do I already know that I have not yet admitted to myself?

I ended up leaving that Iron Butterfly 8-track tape in the glovebox when I sold the Lincoln, but I did soon regret doing this.

For as much as I hate over-analyzing every decision in my life, I found that the things I did too hastily were often the ones that I later regretted, like letting that one tape get away.

It was right after this happened that I stopped viewing my overthinking things as a problem, just because I do it differently than the way other people make decisions. I came to accept that this is just my nature and not a flaw in my character. I just need this type of clarity.

Another good step toward liking myself? I hope so.

With the money I got for the Lincoln, I bought a good used El Camino for a fraction of the price. It was much more practical for hauling personal possessions. Even my bike would fit in the back, if necessary.

I didn't owe a dime on the Mark IV, so the rest of the money would tide me over at school for a good while. Back then semesters were priced in the hundreds of dollars, not the many thousands of dollars like they are today.

I had no plans to bring my bike to school with me, so I rode it over to my parents' house, drained the gas and removed the battery, and chained it down to the large steel loop that I had buried in concrete in the floor years ago to keep my bike from ever walking away one night. There it stayed for several years, until I was well out of school.

I said goodbye to Danny and Mike and the rest of the gang at the Arts Center. I had really grown during my brief time there.

College was an adjustment for me, but no more so than for any other freshman, I suppose. I was a few years older than most of the new students, and many there assumed that I was doing some type of postgraduate work. I kept to myself mostly.

I found computer science to be fascinating. I truly had found my calling. As an aptitude test, for example, we were given a half page of new computer language — all made up, not a real one. We were then asked to solve a particular problem within 10 minutes, and with no more than five lines of code. Some couldn't do it at all, some did it in seven lines, but I did it in three lines of code.

I decided that I was going to squeeze every bit of opportunity that I could out of school, so I applied my perfectionist ways to learning as much as possible, often studying for 10 hours at a time on weekends.

As early November rolled around, I called to talk to my Mom one night about the upcoming Thanksgiving holiday. I planned to drive up to New Jersey for two or three days while on break from school. We finalized all the details, and when we were all done catching up my mother said that my sister Kathy was there and she wanted to talk to me for a minute.

Kathy got on the phone, and we exchanged pleasantries for a few minutes. It was then that she said, "I don't know if Mom already told you this, but a package arrived here for you the other day. Should I send it down to you at school? Were you expecting anything important?" she asked.

"No, I'm not expecting anything. I didn't order anything," I said.

"It's not real large, but it's a little heavy," she added.

"Who is it from?" I asked her.

"It says CACK, from Downey California," she said.

"CACK?" I repeated.

"K-A-C," she spelled out. "Do you want me to open it for you to see what it is?"

Just then I realized what it was; it was from Karen. Karen Anne Carpenter — KAC. She loved her abbreviations.

"Ohhh, I remember what that is now," I fibbed. "No, just leave that aside. I'll grab it when I'm up for Thanksgiving. It's nothing urgent," I said.

"Ok, will do. See you soon!" she said as she hung up.

I had no idea what could be in the package, but just knowing that it was from Karen made me smile.

It was just then that I realized that in the last few months, I had somehow managed not to rehash every moment in my mind that she and I had spent together. I was actually thankful for this. Perhaps it was some kind of safety mechanism in my brain? It was only now and then that she came to me in my dreams, during the early morning hours, to wake me from my sleep.

When I did drive up for Thanksgiving, I glanced over to look at the package, but I never picked it up to avoid anyone else getting curious. It was only after everyone had gone to bed that first night there that I left my room to retrieve it. I opened it quietly once I got back to my room.

There, under many layers of paper and packing peanuts, was a leaded crystal picture frame, with the exact black & white photo that I had commented on back at the Holiday Inn. I had completely forgotten Karen's comment about sending me a better one. She had signed it, "With Love, Karen."

The Sunday after Thanksgiving I drove back to school to finish off the rest of the semester. When I got back, I took the photo that Karen gave me while we were together out of its frame and placed it into the crystal frame, just behind her signed copy.

As Christmas approached, I started to waver back and forth over whether to send Karen a Christmas card. The deciding factor was that I thought I should at least acknowledge her gift. So in the end I did send a card with a simple message inside, thanking her for the framed photo.

I didn't hear anything back, but I wasn't entirely surprised. But I had done what I thought was the right thing, so now it was time for me to leave the girl alone.

It was only years later that I would learn that she most likely never saw my card because many of her outside contacts were being filtered by others, all in the name of her perceived best interest.

In January some really cold and snowy weather rolled in, so it was easy to stay inside and lose myself in my studies. The weeks passed quickly. One day early in March, I found a surprise waiting for me in my mailbox. It was a card from Karen.

The cover said, "Sorry I haven't written, but I thought a phone call would be more personal." The inside continued, "of course I didn't call either, but that's another story." Under this Karen had written in parentheses (I know!!! Sorry!!!). She signed it Kasey.

It was a sweet card. I left it up for months. It was only as the end of the semester approached that I thought to pack it away in a safe place before it accidentally disappeared. I still have it.

By early June classes were over and I headed back up north for the summer break.

I wasn't sure what I'd be doing for the summer work-wise, but I knew instinctively that it wouldn't be anything at the Arts Center. Even though it wasn't for this reason, I needn't have worried, the Carpenters were not on the schedule for 1976. As it turned out, their performance in 1975 was the last time that they would ever appear at this venue.

As disco got a firmer hold on the top 40 stations, I had switched over to jazz stations full time, something that I'd always enjoyed as well. It was a month or two before I realized that this change also had the unintended effect of keeping any Carpenters songs from ever turning up on my radio to remind me of her.

By June I did hear about a new Carpenters album, however, "A Kind Of Hush," and a week or so later I found myself at the music store in the Woodbridge Mall picking up a copy. I found the 8-track version, and smiled to myself when I saw that it was *still* not in Quadrasonic.

That didn't matter much anymore, because the cheapy 8-track player hanging below the dash of my El Camino was not really state of the art like the one in my Lincoln. But I did end up listening to her new album for several weeks, on an endless loop.

Within a few days of returning, I got a job as a computer operator for the summer. It was funny how many businesspeople assumed that if you were a programmer, then you must know everything about the *hardware* side as well. This wasn't at all true, but I took advantage of that fact to learn lots and to earn some decent money over the summer.

Most of these temp jobs were second shift, which regular employees didn't want to work. But I didn't care. And it was actually a very good experience for me.

# July 1976

It was about 11:30 PM when my phone rang. Unless it was close family, most people still seemed to observe the 9 PM cutoff for landline calls back then. That probably seems very quaint nowadays. But at this late hour, I thought that it must be some type of emergency. I had a bit of a lump in my throat when I answered.

"Hello?" I said.

"Oh, good, you're there," I heard a voice say.

"Karen?" I asked, quite surprised.

"Yes, it's me. I'm *sorry*. I hope I didn't wake you. I know it's quite late," she said.

"No, I just got in from work a few minutes ago. You didn't wake me," I said.

Karen continued, "I've been meaning to call … but I'm always running around, and when I think of it, I can't do it, and when I have time to do it, it's always a bad time. It feels like months go by this way. I was sitting here tonight thinking about you, and I just said, 'Screw it, I'm calling.' It feels so good to hear your voice. I'm sorry that I haven't called in so …"

"Shhh," I said. "You're here now. That's all I care about."

"I'm glad," she said. "Me, too."

"And before I forget," I said, "that was such a sweet gift you sent me last year — the framed photo. Thank you."

"I'm glad you liked it," she said. "I know you preferred that particular photo. It hardly feels like much of a gift, but I thought it might at least make you smile."

"It was perfect," I said. "And turning up at my mother's house like that added a little mystery to it all, because it was a few weeks before I could open it."

"Well, I wanted to surprise you, so I didn't want to call and ask for a good mailing address, you being at school and everything. So I got hold of your old boss, Mike, at the Arts Center and asked him. Your friend, Danny, is the one who suggested I mail it to your mom's house, and he gave me the address, along with this phone number," she said.

"When they told me it was heavy I wasn't sure what it could possibly be, so I didn't risk asking anyone else to open it. But it was the crystal frame that made it so heavy. I can't believe you remembered," I said.

"And I got a chuckle out of the card you sent me a few months ago too," I added.

"I'm glad," Karen said. "So, how have you *been*? How's school treating you?"

"Oh, I'm good I guess. I'm learning lots. I think I may have finally found my calling with this computer stuff. It seems to mesh with my crazy brain," I said.

"I love that crazy brain of yours. You taught me a lot. Really. It sounds like you're finally putting that 'gift' of yours to good use," she said.

"Oh, yes, our music conversation. You're sweet to remember that," I replied.

"I remember everything ..." Karen said.

I got a little choked up just then, but I managed to add, "Probably because the sound of my singing etched that whole conversation into your brain."

"Stop!" she laughed. "It wasn't *that* bad," she said. "Not really, I mean. And besides ... I hardly *ever* tell that story to anyone anymore. No one believes me!" she added with a chuckle.

"You stinker," I said with a laugh.

"You always could make me laugh and feel better," she said. "I sure miss that."

After a few seconds of silence, I asked her, "So, what about you? Still running around like usual? How's the travel this year?"

"I'm *trying* to be better about that. I don't have you around to recharge my batteries you know. I'm kind'a pooped," she said.

"As much as I wish I was there, I'm not sure it would be enough anymore. The changes,[31] even since last summer. I'm so worried about you," I said.

"Thank you for worrying, but I'm working on it all, really," she said.

"Karen I wish that there was a single thing I could do to help, but it's all on you," I said.

"I do understand these things," she said. "It's difficult to explain, but sometimes I feel like I'm watching my life on TV, but I have no control over the program."

"I know that you're doing the best you can," I said.

"I'm really trying. Thank you," she said.

Thinking it time to change the subject, I asked, "So how are things going with you and Terry? Finally get that TV installed for yourself over there?"

"No, that was probably a bad idea on my part. The whole relationship, I mean. I moved in with him for a very short while and I was going crazy. That's when I called it quits. We're over," she said.

---

31 Karen suffered from what would later be well known as anorexia nervosa, an eating disorder characterized by an abnormally low body weight, a fear of gaining weight, and a distorted perception of weight. It causes you to control calorie intake by vomiting after eating or by misusing laxatives, diet aids, diuretics, or enemas. It's an extremely unhealthy and sometimes life-threatening way to try to cope with emotional problems. When you have anorexia, you often equate thinness with self-worth.

"I'm sorry to hear that, but I think you did it for all the right reasons," I said.

"I think so, too," she added.

"I finished up that apartment I told you about. We ended up merging two units into one new big one," Karen said.

"Oh, that's wonderful! Did you end up needing that separate stuffed animal room?" I teased her.

Karen just laughed and said "*No!*"

"Well, I'm happy for you," I said. "How has Richard been with all your plans? I mean is everything ok there? I read about the whole 'Sedaka' thing last year."

"Oh, I still feel awful about all of that. I was so upset," Karen replied.

"Well, from what I read, it wasn't your decision," I said.

"No, it wasn't," she said. "But Rich was always fine with all my plans. He was never the problem. My *mother* was the problem."

As if she were putting off this question for as long as possible, she finally asked, "Have you been listening to the new recordings?"

"Oh, of course," I said. "I got your newest album as soon as I heard about it."

A bit hesitantly, she asked, "So what did you think of *our* song?"

As much as I wondered if this question might ever come up one day, when it actually did I just froze inside, not knowing what to say. After several seconds the delay became obvious.

Without waiting for an answer, Karen came back much more forcefully this time, "Come on, man, don't pretend like you don't know what I'm talking about. You were there."

"I… I thought it was the most beautiful song I've ever heard," I replied. "I wasn't pretending that I didn't know. Honest. I was just a little choked up and couldn't speak. As beautiful as that song is, it brings back so many memories for me that it can be difficult to handle sometimes," I said.

Karen said nothing, as she let me finish.

"I don't know how you managed to get so many things into that song. The first time that I heard it I was just knocked out, not knowing that it was even written. It was so perfect," I said.

After a few second's pause, Karen replied, "I supplied the hook. I did it very casually, so that the guys would pick up on it. And it worked … they thought they were so brilliant to think of it. I'm not a songwriter, so I had no idea what they could do with the perfection line and all the other things I said, but they made it work even better than I could have hoped for. They're so good.

"Once they got rolling with it, I suggested a few other small tweaks along the way … the important parts anyway. I knew you'd recognize it," she said.

A few seconds later she added, "It's a difficult song for me to do sometimes. Not just in the studio, even on stage. I get a little choked up myself, too, at times. But it's absolutely my favorite song that we've ever done."

"You sing it beautifully," I replied.

I had to pause for a moment, feeling a little overwhelmed. It wasn't an awkward silence, however, since I think we were both feeling the same way.

After a few seconds, I said, "I was really hoping that you would have taken my hint to do that Gary Puckett song we talked about on the new album too. Remember? I just have a feeling that it would be a big hit for you. As a fan I mean. Well ... *maybe* some other time," I said, starting to feel awkward for bringing it up again, after all this time.

"Over You?" Karen said. "I didn't forget. I went out and got a recording of it as soon as we got back to California. It *is* a beautiful song. It's amazing how much it reminds me of us, just like the one I recorded," she said.

"I heard it a few months ago, probably for the first time since we were together," I said. "I was thinking the same thing. It was just a song that I loved when I told you about it, but it's even more special to me now."

"I let Rich have a listen to it a few weeks after we got back from the tour. He thought that he might be able to make it work for us. But as soon as it came out somehow that you were involved in suggesting it, the song kinda fell off the radar. I'm sorry, I know you were looking forward to it. I very much wanted to sing it for you," she said.

"Thank you. I understand, I guess," I said. "I don't think that he has ever forgiven me for taking you out on my motorcycle. That and a dozen other things, I'm sure."

After another pause, Karen said, "But about that Gary Puckett song …" she said softly. "Are you?" and a second later "… *over* me?" she asked.

She didn't have to finish the sentence. I knew what she was asking the moment she started to speak. I felt like I was being crushed by the weight of the world.

I replied, "Karen, getting over you is the hardest thing I've ever had to do."

I could feel the tension over the line. "You *are*?" she said slowly, almost in shock.

"No … no I'm *not*," I said. "I mean it's the hardest thing I've ever *tried* to do. I couldn't do it. Deep down I don't think I even want to. If you asked me today, would I rather live with the heartache and keep the memories, or erase the memory and lose the pain, I'd still pick you."

After a moment Karen said, "There's my guy. Always looking at things a hundred different ways. But, thanks … thank you for that. You always looked at me in a way that no one else ever has. Special, I mean. And I could feel it every time you caught my eye and just smiled."

"You'll always be special to me, Karen," I said.

After an awkward silence she said, "Well… it's getting late. I should probably let you get some sleep," and after another pause she said, "Goodbye, John."

"You take care, Kasey," I replied.

I sat there and thought about Karen for a long while after I hung up the phone. It felt as though I had reached the last page of a wonderful book, and it was time to close the back cover.

So as much as it was a very sad moment for me, I was also left with a lot of wonderful memories. But it was definitely time to move on with my life.

After hanging up the phone on her end, Karen slowly got up and walked over to the stereo. She pulled an album off the shelf, and after studying the jacket for a moment, she took out the record inside. She reached down to the player, flicked on a switch, and placed the record on the turntable.

As she sat back down in the chair, she turned off the light on the end table. The room was dark, and she was illuminated only by the setting sun outside her window.

There was the click of a lighter and the glow of a cigarette as Karen inhaled. She reached over to pick up a glass of wine from the end table. Her elbow was resting on the arm of the chair as she held the glass in the air.

There was a slight crunch sound from the speakers as the needle finally landed on the vinyl record. Gary Puckett began singing "Over You" on the stereo.

As she listened in the dark, tears started running down her cheek. She sat there motionless, while the song continued to play.

This song is an important part of the story. To hear this song, scan the QR code with your smartphone camera and click the link that appears.

"Over You." Gary Puckett & The Union Gap, 1968.

# Moving On

After the summer break I returned to school for year number two. It was almost a complete redo of the first year. Wake up, school, study, sleep, repeat.

I wish that there was something memorable to even talk about, but all those next three years just droned on by. I did receive an excellent education, however, which was the point, so it was all worth it.

I ended up finishing school with a 3.98 grade point average. And it should have been 4.0, but for one instructor who announced on our first day of class that she never gave A's. I killed myself in that class and still ended up with a B. And it wasn't even a computer class, just some English Lit course. I was so miffed that I re-enrolled to take that same class again the next semester.

It didn't occur to me for a moment that I would draw the exact same instructor! But I did. After the first day, I never returned, and I got an incomplete-F for the class. Thank goodness the school only counted the highest grade for duplicates. I decided to just let it go. This was the instructor's issue. I didn't want it to be mine.

Once I finished school, I found out the same hard truth that so many other graduates discover: without programming experience, no one wants to hire you. And you can't get experience without being hired!

But I had one card to play that most folks didn't. In the end it was the routine computer operator work that I did that first summer and each summer thereafter that gave me a foot in the door.

By this point I had experience with a whole range of IBM and UNIX systems. I rewrote my resume to emphasize the operations side, and within a few weeks I started working full time at a Fortune 500 pharmaceutical company as a computer operator. After about a year of paying my dues in this way, I was able to apply internally for a junior programmer position, and I got it.

The usual rule of thumb at the time was that it took you about two years to master 90% of each job level. This seemed to track about right for me. Every other year I found myself looking forward to that next promotion — not so much for the additional money, which was always welcomed — but more that by the end of that two year cycle, I was starting to get bored with my current job and I needed a new challenge.

And so I moved up over the years: first to full programmer, then programmer analyst, then over to database analyst for something completely new, and then to project manager, then manager. Each level provided a new challenge, despite the fact that I was slowly starting to shift from the technical side over to the management side.

All during school and my early work career, I would see Karen now and then on some Carpenters TV special, as a guest on the "Tonight Show," or in some magazine article about them. Only one interview that I remember from back then caused me to really worry about her, however. I don't even recall the exact nature of the question, but it was her *answer* that gave me pause.

She said something to the effect "... we give them something traditional and they don't want it. We give them something experimental and they don't want it. If someone would just tell us what the problem is, we'll take care of it."

She was speaking about recent recordings. I sensed a trace of desperation in her words. I was worried that the Carpenters as a group had run its course and was on the decline and that they were struggling to keep their album sales and audience. By this point they had already enjoyed years-more success than many other recording artists, so it was very possible.

But if Karen was still dependent on that audience fix that she once told me about, I was worried that it may not be there for her anymore, at least not in the way that she needed.

And she kept getting so painfully thin.

Then one day in 1980 I read of Karen's upcoming marriage. So, it was official. My last remaining dream bubble had burst ... I'd really lost her — forever.

# January 11, 1983

As I remember, it was right around 6 PM that day when the phone rang, and I picked it up to say hello.

"Hey, *you …*" I heard, and after another second, "Remember *me*?"

"Karen?" I said. "Wow, what a wonderful surprise."

"I wasn't sure if you'd know who it was. It's been way too many years," she said.

"Oh, of course. How could I forget you," I said. "It's so great to hear your voice. How *are* you?"

"I can't complain, I guess," she said. "And you, everything ok there?" she asked.

"Yes, I'm doing good here, too, just taking it one day at a time," I replied. "I haven't seen your name in the papers in a while. What have you been up to? Finally taking it easy, I hope? "

"Something like that …" she replied, offering no more.

After a short pause, I said, "You were so beautiful in the wedding photos that I saw a few years ago. You still have that same perfect smile."

"Oh, thank you," she said. She sighed. "Boy, that seems like a million years ago, so much has happened."

"Bad?" I asked.

"Well, the reception was probably the best part of the marriage, if that tells you anything. It has been a disaster. Probably the biggest mistake of my life," she said.

"Oh, I'm so sorry. I thought you had finally found your happiness," I said.

"No, it was over almost as soon as it started," she said. "For all my worries about finding someone who checked off all the right boxes, I didn't factor in being completely deceived. I'm such a fool sometimes. We're actually finalizing the divorce right now. It should all be over in a few weeks."

"I'm so sorry," I said again.

"What can ya do," she said. "You probably won't hear too much about it because part of the agreement was that neither party disclose any details. So, hopefully, it'll blow over in a day or two with the press."

"Oh, I hope so, for your sake," I said.

After a brief pause, I said, "Karen, can I say something to you before I lose my nerve. Not moving to California back in 1975 was the biggest mistake of *my* life. I've been sorting through a lot of old issues lately … my issues, I mean. And I really think that I was wrong not to have given us a chance back then. Maybe I didn't have all the paper lists like you did, but I guess I had my own rules in my head about what should or shouldn't be, and they got in the way of *my* life, too. But there really is no such thing as perfection when it comes to relationships, and I was wrong to want to wait for it," I said.

"You're sweet to think that … you really are. But it wasn't a mistake. I've had a long string of failed relationships since then that says you were exactly right," she said. "I would never want you to be on that list of failures. I'd rather remember the good times."

"You can't consider these things failures," I said. "Finding the right person is like shopping for a new dress. Is it a failure if it looks nice, but it doesn't fit you? Not at all. You just keep looking. I mean there's more to it than this of course, but that's really the big picture."

"There's my guy," she said. "Always looking at things a hundred different ways. But this is way different."

After a short pause, she continued, "You were right back then. I *was* broken. And I never found a healthy way to deal with *any* of it. Things just kept getting worse. My life seemed to bounce back and forth between setbacks and bad decisions, in an endless downward spiral. You would have been chewed up in my wake, just like everyone else. But after my solo album got shelved[32] and my marriage tanked, I hit bottom. I really scared myself."

After another second she added, "But I don't want to die."

---

[32] Karen Carpenter started recording her solo album in New York City in 1979. The finished product was very different from the usual Carpenters material, with more mature lyrics and songs that took better advantage of Karen's vocal range. The album received a tepid response from Richard Carpenter and A&M executives when they heard the finished material in early 1980, and it was shelved by A&M Records. A&M subsequently charged Karen $400,000 ($1.7 million in 2024 dollars) to cover the cost of recording her unreleased album, to be paid out of the duo's future royalties.

"Karen!" I said, as I was filled with panic.

"Shhh … don't worry," she said. "Even I couldn't ignore it any longer. I've been getting help all this past year. Real help. I've been seeing a doctor in New York City, and I think it might be working this time. I've already gained 20 pounds, and I'm starting to feel a little better too."

"Oh, thank goodness," I said. "I saw you on TV about two years ago, and you looked so frail. I was heartbroken for you. But I wish I knew that you were so close all that time. I would have come to visit you."

"No, I wouldn't have wanted you to see me. Not like that," she said.

"But that's actually the reason why I'm calling today," she said. "I'm thinking about heading to New York again sometime later in March, once a few more things are wrapped up out here. It would be so good for us to get together while I'm out there and catch up, maybe over a drink or something? Would that be ok?"

"Yes, I'd love that," I replied.

Feeling more confident, she continued, "Or if it's not a crazy busy time for you, maybe we can even make a long weekend out of it. To really have some time to relax and talk, like we did that summer? I could really use that." She stopped just then. "I'm sorry, that sounded selfish."

"I understand exactly what you mean. And you're more than welcome to stay here for as long as you can," I said.

"Thank you," she replied.

She paused again. "A long time ago you said that if you ever sorted out a few things in your life, that you'd come looking for me just as fast as you could. Well, this is me, coming back to look for you ...

"I'm not saying that it's even possible, or that it's something that either one of us might still want for that matter. But I'd sure like to find out if it is ... Those days together seem like the most normal time in my life since this music stuff started. Perfect, actually.

"And it's not just me imagining things that didn't happen, because you were there, too. That's why I can't think of anyone else I'd rather spend some time with right now, to just talk," she said.

"I would love that, Karen," I said.

"Oh, I'm so glad," she said. "I was *so* afraid to ask. I was sure that too much time had passed."

"No ... never. I can't wait to see you," I said.

"Me, too, you," she said.

"And who knows, maybe we'll even have time to drive out to Sandy Hook while I'm there. We did a lot of good talking out there on the beach. But this time we'll bring along a beach blanket, *you know*, for protection. To keep the sand out of your car," she added.

"You're still my number one buster," I replied.

It was just about this point that I heard a noise on her side of the line.

"Oh, damn," she said. "They're calling me from the lobby. My car must be here early. I thought I had enough time to talk to you while I was waiting. They're doing a promotional thing for the Grammys this evening, and Rich and I are attending. I'm sorry. I have to go. But I promise that I'll call you in a few weeks, once some things are wrapped up out here, and I have some firm dates for you, ok?"

"I can't wait. Later, *you*," I said.

"You, *too* ... bye!" Karen said, as she hung up the phone.

# March 20, 1983, 9 PM

"That was going to be the last time that I would ever talk to Karen," I said to Kathy. "The Grammys promo that day was the last public event she would ever attend. The group photo from that evening may even be her last public photo. I don't really know.

"A few weeks after we talked, she woke up one Friday morning, went down to the kitchen to turn on the coffee pot, and went back to her bedroom. It was there that she was found on the floor unconscious, a short while later.

"She passed away that morning from cardiac arrest," I said.

"The years of self-starvation had destroyed her health. They said later that her heart simply died. This was just last month, February 4th. She was only 32 years old," I added.

As I said this a look of shock came over my sister's face, and she reached out and put her left hand on my shoulder.

"Oh, my God. I did hear about that last month. I completely forgot about it. Oh, that's so horrible," she said.

I stood up and walked over to the dresser a few feet away and opened the top drawer. I took out a folded magazine that I had put in there earlier, while cleaning up.

I turned back around to the bed where Kathy was still seated, and I put the magazine down in front of her.

As I let go of the magazine it unfolded to reveal Karen on the cover of People magazine.

"She was supposed to sign her divorce papers the afternoon of the day she died," I said.

My sister stood up and gave me a long hug, and we just stood there for a moment or two. It was only the sound of the TV from the other room that brought us both back to reality.

In all this time, we had completely forgotten about Bill, as we were both so engrossed in the story.

Just then my sister turned back toward the bed and picked up the People magazine to read the cover. After a moment her head suddenly turned back toward me, as though she just thought of something.

"I didn't want to interrupt your story earlier to ask, but what was the song that Karen talked to you about singing back in 1976, I think? The one she called 'our' song, meaning yours and hers?" she asked.

I looked at my sister for a moment, and then I turned back toward the still-open dresser drawer. I took out a cassette tape player, placed it on top of the dresser, and closed the drawer.

"I've been listening to it a lot these last few weeks," I said.

I reached over and pressed <PLAY> on the cassette player.

As the song "I Need To Be In Love" started, memories of my time together with Karen back in 1975 started flooding through my mind one more time. They always made me feel warm inside.

I love you Kasey … pinky swear.

- The End -

This song is an important part of the story. To hear this song, scan this QR code with your smartphone camera and click the link that appears on the screen.

"I Need To Be In Love." Carpenters, 1976.

# Epilogue

Karen's death finally erased any hope that may have lingered to ever be with her again. And her loss was only made worse by the knowledge that she was wondering if another try might be possible. I'll never know what would have happened if we did. Would I have been just another one of those bad decisions that she quickly came to regret? Would the seven years of life experiences since our time together have left her spirit unrecognizable to me? Or would we have just made each other happy, just as we had so long ago, with each of us giving the other the love and support that was missing in our lives?

I don't know any of these things.

But I *do* know that when we talked on the phone, I still heard that same sweet kid I met in 1975. And she still had that same level of trust in me that I had somehow earned that day at Sandy Hook — and the confidence to share some of her innermost thoughts and feelings. And this was a damn good start.

I only wish that we had the chance to find out.

But I *was* thankful that we got to talk one last time before she journeyed on.

I dated very little for almost four years after she passed. This was never a conscious decision on my part, but more the end result of doing very little about it each and every day of those four years.

There were the occasional dinners with someone from the office or other people I met. I knew enough to know that I should *want* to, but in the end I never seriously pursued anyone. I'm sure that they assumed I wasn't interested. And I suppose that's because I wasn't.

It was one Labor Day picnic at my brother's house that would finally break this cycle. I met one of his coworkers there. Beth. She had a wonderful smile, a delightful sense of humor, and a razor sharp wit. We talked effortlessly for hours, moving from one topic to another. I found myself completely charmed by her. By the end of the picnic, I had asked her out for the following weekend, and she said yes.

We dated for a few weeks, and things were always just as fun and effortless. But the relationship went nowhere. Eventually I discovered that she was in love with a married man, and he couldn't reciprocate. So, while she considered herself single and free to date, the reality was that she had already given her heart away to someone else.

I was a bit crushed by this, because she was the first person since Karen who had really interested me — a lot.

But I soon came to appreciate that this whole experience was just life's way of giving me a wakeup call. My world had been empty for far too many years, and it was time for a change.

Over the next two years I made an active effort to meet new people, and I did. Sometimes just a single date, and other times for a few months before we decided to part. But after a long search, I finally found someone. She was smart and beautiful. Way out of my league. We dated for about 10 months before moving in together. We bought a house and eventually married.

We had many years of happiness. In most respects our tastes were almost identical. We became more than husband and wife; we were also best friends. We did have our occasional disagreements, as every couple does, but we always managed to work through them. We were never completely compatible, but I wondered if any couple truly is. Marriage is not easy, and it requires commitment and work to be successful.

By this point in my career I had progressed to IT director at work, an officer of the company. But the politics at this level were cutthroat. At first I chose not to play that game, but I soon discovered that if you are not at the table, then you are on the menu.

A year or so into my new job a vice president made a play to have me removed from my position so that it could be given to his wife, who was one of my managers. I didn't know it when I accepted the job, but he had already done this once before, to the person who held my job before me.

But despite his best efforts, his wife was passed over that time, and the job was given to me. And rightly so; she was woefully unqualified. Her single greatest talent seemed to be knowing when to step aside to give others around her a better view of the fan before the shit hit it.

In the end, everyone involved took a hit to their careers. I was reminded of something Karen had told me years ago, about how all the good things about her job were slowly being stripped away. That's how I felt too, about my work.

But it was the stress of these last few years that took its worst toll on me. For my entire career I attended meetings and never took notes. I memorized everything. I made occasional scribbles on my pad only to appear to be paying attention, but I threw these away after the meetings. But by the end of several years of political battles, my memory skills were fading fast. Way too much stress, which I never handled well.

Not only did I now have to write everything down, there were times when I didn't even recall the *meeting* without some reminders!

And my music skills? I would still smile knowingly after the first few notes. "I know that one," I would think to myself. But no song titles ever came to mind anymore.

This was all very bad.

My wife was under similar stress, having achieved a senior spot in her career as well. By this point we had a second home in Virginia right on the Chesapeake Bay at it's widest point, virtually an ocean view. Relaxing there for a few days every couple of weeks seemed to be the only thing keeping us sane.

Eventually, for the sake of our health, we both decided to quit our jobs, sell our New Jersey home, and move full time to the waterfront house. Our New Jersey house sold just six weeks before the housing market crash of 2006. We just missed it.

The move was an adjustment for both of us. I started over with my own small business. But despite the business growing each year, I was starting from almost nothing, and we were now in the midst of the great recession. Over time, our savings were eventually depleted fixing up the Virginia house, and we were just living month to month.

Then there was the strain of being eight hours away from loved ones. My wife sometimes spent a month at a time in New Jersey, taking care of family members.

For the next 10 years we seemed to be in a slow downward spiral, to the point where all the good things were forgotten and only the problems and incompatibility issues between us remained. It's always a sin when you reach this point, because sometimes a relationship can get so broken that it can't be fixed. But this takes two, and I accept responsibility for my share of the hurt. We eventually divorced.

In all these years I still thought of Karen now and then, usually when an old Carpenters song came on the radio. And she always made me smile. But I was always careful to only think about the good times. I avoided the ABC Karen Carpenter Story when it came out in 1989, and I have never seen it to this day.

And this is how it remained for decades.

It was only during the Covid lockdowns of the 2020's that I ran across a three-part documentary about the Carpenters and Karen's life on YouTube by Justin Root while watching some old music videos there. I opened it hesitantly at first, ready to cancel it at any moment. But I was drawn in by what I saw. It was excellent. The video prompted me to buy the book "Little Girl Blue" by Randy Schmidt. Both are highly recommended.

While many of the things I learned made me smile, I was also saddened by too many other details of her life. Karen had actually wanted to cancel her wedding only a few days before it was to happen, having just learned something disturbing about her future husband. Karen's mother wouldn't let her do it for the sake of appearances. The whole world was watching after all.

I thought back to the several times Karen told me that she had no control over anything in her life, but she didn't even have control over her own life.

And when I learned the depth of her eating disorder — that she was down to 77 pounds at one point, my heart broke for her. She would take up to 80 Dulcolax tablets a day to lose weight.

Her husband simply referred to her as "a bag of bones."

Karen hid so much pain behind that beautiful smile, but in the end it was all too much for anyone to bear.

I have never been a big one for regrets, because in reality we're all just doing the best that we can every day with what we know how to do. To me it makes as much sense as beating yourself up for not having known today's winning lottery numbers yesterday and buying yourself a ticket.

But at the same time, I often muse that what passes for wisdom may just be knowing enough not to make the same mistake more than once.

So while I can't say that I regret how things worked out with Karen and me, I might add one final thought: If I ever did get those three wishes that I talked to her about so many years ago, my *second* wish would be to go back to that summer of 1975, and say *Yes* to a dream.

Before I walk away from my keyboard for the last time, I hope that I may be granted one final indulgence and share this last song. I rediscovered it only recently. But to me it conveys in three minutes the feelings that all these many pages have tried so hard to describe.

Karen was right that one day so many years ago. "Country" does good love songs, too.

-
- JML -

To hear this song, scan this QR code with your smartphone camera and click the link that appears on the screen.

"I Wouldn't Have Missed It For The World." Ronnie Milsap, 1981. Craft Recordings, a division of Concord Music Group. All rights reserved.

# Supplemental

Candid photo of Karen on stage, circa 1974.
Previously unpublished.

Garden State Arts Center open air Stage

John's Harley-Davidson Superglide,
seen here in 2006

John's autographed program
from 1973

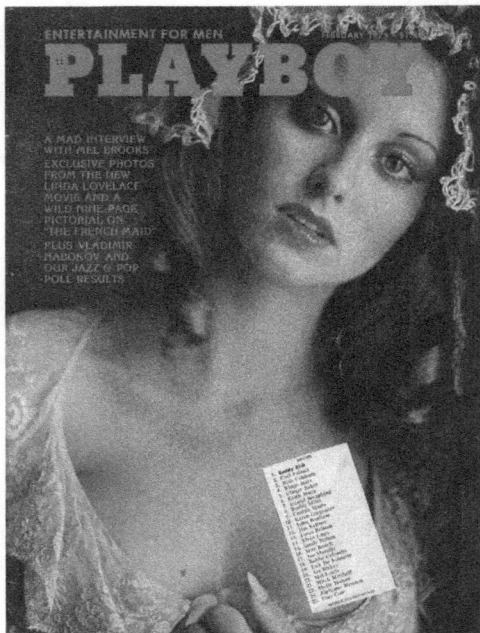

Karen ranked #10 on the Feb. 1975
Playboy top 25 drummer list

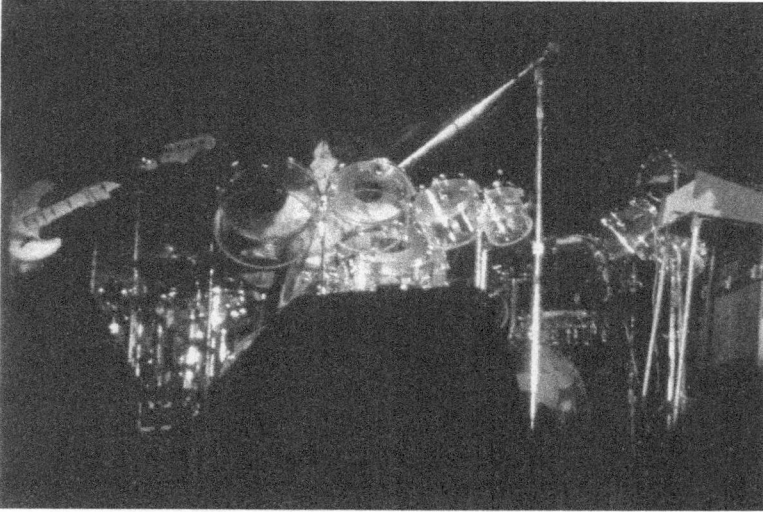

Karen enjoying her drums. Previously unpublished photo.
CarpentersLegacy.com

Sandy Hook, New Jersey

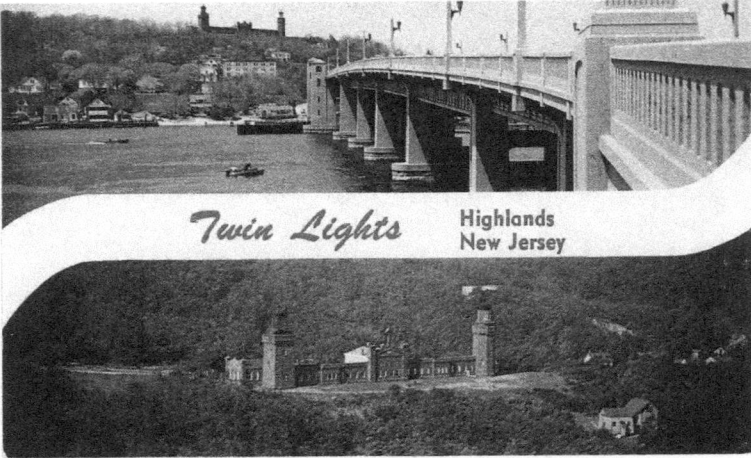

Parlin Color Co

The Twin Lights, and the old drawbridge to Sandy Hook, which was
replaced several decades later

Ford Motor Company

John's Continental Mark IV, which was voted America's most
beautiful car when it was first introduced

The Seaside Heights boardwalk at night

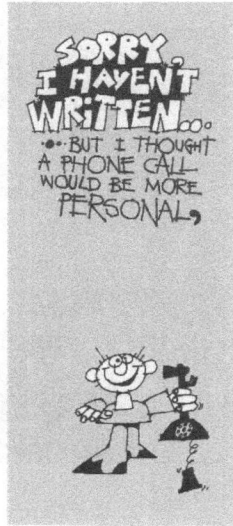

SORRY, I HAVEN'T WRITTEN... ••• BUT I THOUGHT A PHONE CALL WOULD BE MORE PERSONAL,

John's favorite photograph of
Karen, autographed by her

Karen's card to John

Karen Anne Carpenter   1950 - 1983

"Eve" Carpenters, 1969.

To hear this song, scan the QR code with your smartphone camera
and click the link that appears on the screen.

"Goodbye To Love" Carpenters, 1972.

To hear this song, scan the QR code with your smartphone camera and
click the link that appears on the screen.

"Take Five" The Dave Brubeck Quartet, 1959.

To hear this song, scan the QR code with your smartphone camera and
click the link that appears on the screen.

"Wipe Out" The Surfaris, 1963.

To hear this song, scan the QR code with your smartphone camera and click the link that appears on the screen.

"In-A-Gadda-Da-Vida." Iron Butterfly, 1968.

To hear this song, scan the QR code with your smartphone camera and click the link that appears on the screen.